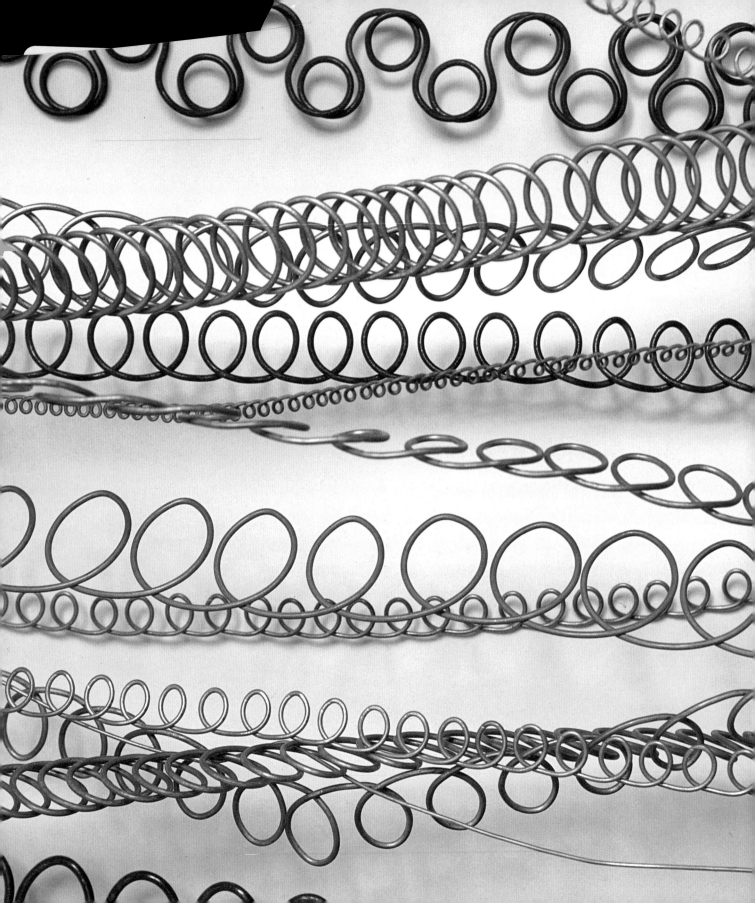

EVERYDAY THINGS

WIRE

DESIGN
STAFFORD CLIFF

STUDIO PHOTOGRAPHY
MARC SCHWARTZ

TEXT

SUZANNE SLESIN
DANIEL ROZENSZTROCH

LOCATION
PHOTOGRAPHY
GILLES DE CHABANEIX

EVERYDAY THINGS

WIRE

SUZANNE SLESIN
DANIEL ROZENSZTROCH
JEAN-LOUIS MENARD
STAFFORD CLIFF
GILLES DE CHABANEIX

ABBEVILLE PRESS
PUBLISHERS

NEW YORK LONDON PARIS

Jacket front: A decorative display of wire kitchen utensils
(see page 39).
Jacket back: A gracefully shaped wire fruit basket (see page 37).
Endpapers: For an animated film, wire craftsman Ladislav
Mikulik created portraits in wire of the people in Senica, a
Slovakian village, including this tinker.

Editor: Jacqueline Decter
Art Director: Monika Keano
Production Editor: Owen Dugan
Production Manager: Simone René

Library of Congress Cataloging-in-Publication Data

Wire / Suzanne Slesin ... [et al.].
p. cm. — (Everyday things)
Includes index.
ISBN 1-55859-792-1
1. Wire in interior decoration. 2. Wire craft.
I. Slesin, Suzanne. II. Series.
NK2115.5.W57W57 1994
747'.9—dc2 94-11054

A hundred-year-old wire bird cage topped with a cupola reflects the eclectic taste in architecture that was favored at the turn of the century. Thin wire was particularly suitable for crafting bird cages and was easily wrought into fanciful abodes. A white dove is the current occupant of this palatial birdhouse.

PREFACE

One day about five years ago, on an early-morning foray to a small flea market in L'Isle-sur-la-Sorgue in Provence, we happened upon a wire salad basket, sort of like the ones that were used in the kitchens of our childhood. But this one was somehow different. We don't know if it was its elegant shape or the decorative detail on its handle, but we suddenly realized that this simple, everyday object was anything but ordinary.

A few weeks later, in the window of a fancy antiques shop in Paris, we were surprised to see an extravagantly crafted basket, also made of ordinary wire. Its multitude of tassels, its double monogram, and its complex motifs of woven wire made it exceptional. Yet as a basket for croissants and brioches that had probably sat for years on the marble counter of the neighborhood patisserie, it was also an object that had once led an ordinary life.

That was the beginning of our fascination with wire. The search was on, but because things made of wire tend to be thrown away without a thought when they rust after years of loyal service in the kitchen, wine cellar, laundry, or garden, there were not many pieces to be found. Nevertheless, we kept looking and developed a sixth sense for ferreting out wire things. From potato mashers and eggbeaters to rococo candelabras and Victorian bird cages, our collection grew. The larger it became, the more we realized what an important role wire had played in many different countries and professions. And we marveled at the variety of practical, imaginative, and charming forms a material so plain could take.

We had become avid collectors. But it was only when the curator of the Bibliothèque Forney, a decorative arts library in Paris, invited us to exhibit our wire pieces that we started to look into their roots. Like the objects themselves, their history had also been neglected, if not forgotten.

In 1991, while traveling through remote mountain villages in Central Europe, we were surprised to see how many wire utensils were still in use in rural homes. Coincidentally a Slovakian friend, leafing through a local newspaper, came upon an article about the Považské Museum in Žilina, which specialized in wire.

Back in the United States in the months that followed a special trip to Žilina, we continued our obsessive search for wire at flea markets and antiques shows. Our bounty included the same type of florists' topiary forms that we had seen in Slovakia as well as ingenious American-made hangers, carpet beaters, and clam baskets.

Wire has entwined our love for folk art with our life-long curiosity about everyday things: a fascination with ordinary objects that time and new sensibilities have transformed into the extraordinary.

RIGHT In Bratislava, Ladislav Jurovaty, one of the last tinkers to maintain the tradition of wirework in Slovakia, dexterously repairs a piece of local pottery.

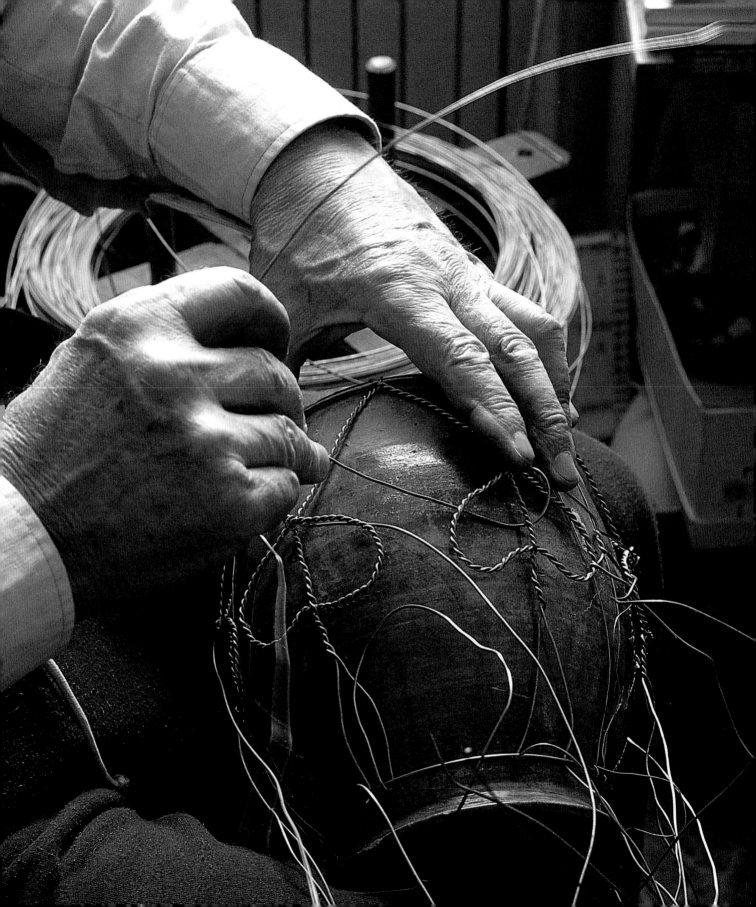

LEFT Wire has been used to repair the broken spongeware pots and painted platter that are part of a collection of the Stará Ľubovňa Open-Air Museum in Slovakia.

RIGHT An eighteenth-century jar, one of the oldest pieces of its kind to survive, is in the Považské Museum in Žilina. Like many other everyday objects, it was repaired with wire.

HISTORY

The story of wire objects begins in seventeenth-century Slovakia, where thin strands of laminated iron forged by ironmongers were first used to repair broken pottery. It was a time of famine and misery in the rural areas, and some people who became known as tinkers would use wire to repair their own few pieces or to fix someone else's broken bowl or pitcher in exchange for a meal.

Little by little, wirework developed into a trade throughout northern Slovakia, and tinkers were recognized as being part of a bona fide profession. By the end of the eighteenth century tinkering had become an important activity in many villages. Slovakian tinkers had already traveled all over the Austro-Hungarian Empire and beyond, disseminating their craft and selling the everyday objects they made out of wire.

Some prospered and returned to their homeland. Others settled in foreign countries, especially Russia, Germany, France, and America, where they adapted their craft to a new and more demanding clientele. Wire animal traps, spoons, ladles, colanders, baskets, and muzzles gave way to more refined frames, vases, fruit stands, bottle carriers, and toys.

As a craft, wireworking reached its height at the turn of the century when ten thousand tinkers were working in Europe and America. New technological advances in metalwork now allowed the most talented among the craftsmen to express themselves in an artistic manner that had little to do with the utilitarian objects that had been their original stock-in-trade.

At the same time many workshops were established to produce wire objects by hand in greater quantities. In France and the United States a wide range of wire utensils and objects were offered in catalogs and department stores to attract a new generation of consumers. Itinerant peddlers, who sold their wares in the street or at markets, were also instrumental in making inexpensive wire objects available to a wider audience.

Even though many wire pieces were tinned, most were highly susceptible to rust, and they began to fall out of favor when objects made out of more modern materials such as enamel, stainless steel, and eventually plastic came on the market. The production of handmade wire objects ceased almost completely with the onset of World War II. Although a few small

RIGHT In a 1940 photograph taken in the region of Kysuče, Slovakia, near the Polish border, a craftsman still wears the traditional nineteenth-century garb of the tinker, including a heavy linen shirt and felt trousers and tunic. In the summer the tinker walked barefoot, and he always carried a shoulder bag and a roll of wire with him. Považské Museum, Žilina

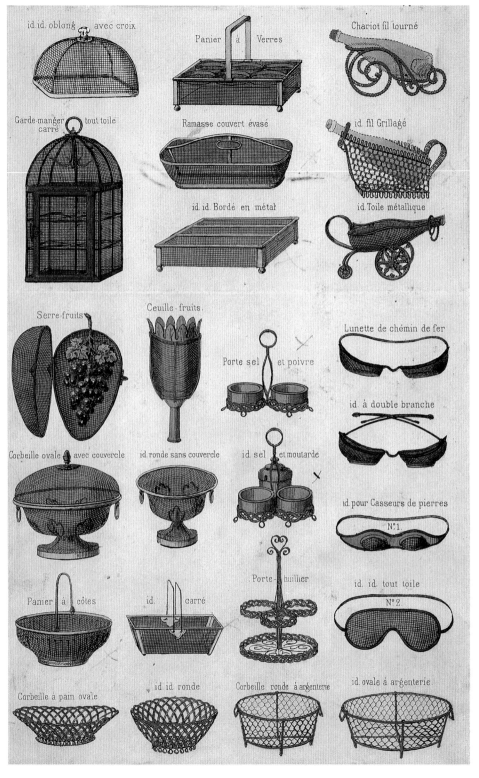

workshops attempted to maintain the older traditions, wireworking as a craft disappeared.

The skill and romance of the wire artisan were immortalized by the famous Austrian composer Franz Lehár in his 1902 operetta *Der Rastelbinder* (The Tinker). Nevertheless, the tinker and his treasure trove of wire were destined to be relegated to history—until now. A renewed appreciation for the tinker's craft has reawakened interest in wire objects as decorative objects and consequently as collectibles.

LEFT AND RIGHT French catalog from the Bellanger-Fasbender company, 1880. Depicted in hand-colored engravings; the wire objects include baskets, wine caddies, condiment sets, grills, toasters, bottle carriers, egg holders, and platters. Bibliothèque Forney, Paris

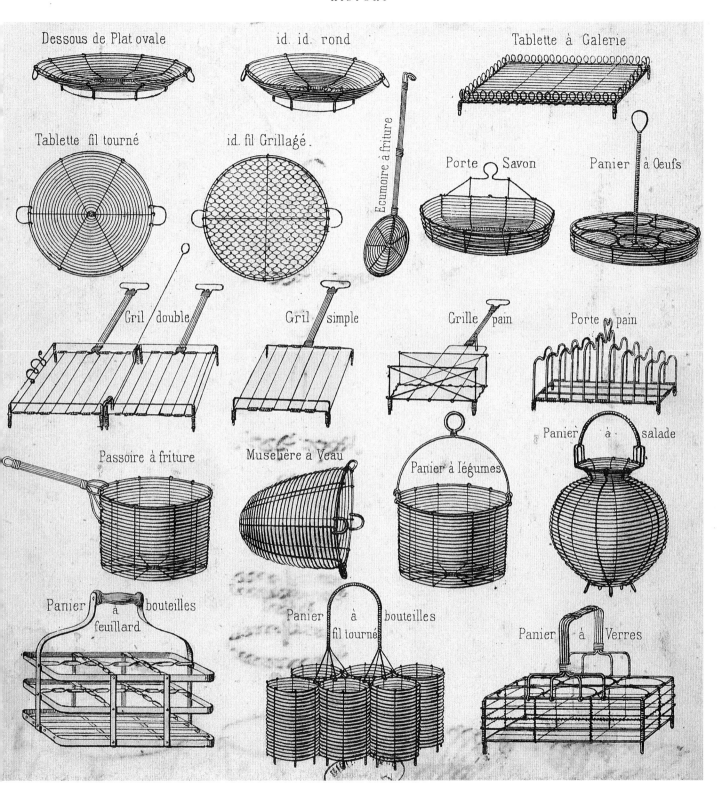

Dessous de Plat ovale

id. id. rond

Tablette à Galerie

Tablette fil tourné

id. fil Grillagé.

Ecumoire à friture

Porte Savon

Panier à Oeufs

Gril double

Gril simple

Grille pain

Porte pain

Passoire à friture

Muselière à Veau

Panier à légumes

Panier à salade

Panier à bouteilles feuillard

Panier à bouteilles fil tourné

Panier à Verres

RIGHT Stephen Raisek stands in front of his florist shop in Chicago, which specialized in wire topiary forms that were usually used for floral tributes at funerals. Raysik Family Photographs, The Balch Institute for Ethnic Studies Library, Philadelphia

BELOW The 1911–12 wholesale catalog from the Baudoin company in Pontoise, near Paris, describes the various wire utensils offered and lists their prices, which depended on size and quantity. Custom orders could also be fulfilled.

OPPOSITE Items available from the wholesale price list of wire floral designs manufactured by John Raysik of Philadelphia include topiary forms in the shape of clocks, crowns, and clover leaves. The Balch Institute for Ethnic Studies, Philadelphia

Articles en fil de fer

172   172 bis

			Nombre de Barres	6	8	10	12	14
162	Grils	carrés doubles forts — douzaine			7.50	9.50	12.	15.
163	„ „	simples ordinaires — „		1.75	2.50	3.50		
164	„ „	forts			3.50	4.70	6.	7.50

			Diamètre	18	20	22	24	26	28	30 m
165	Volettes pâtissiers sans pieds	douzaine		2.20	2.45	2.75	3.	3.25	3.75	4.40
166	„ avec pieds			2.45	2.75	3.	3.25	3.50	4.10	4.60

(Toutes autres dimensions sur demande)

				27x20	30x22	35x24	37x26
167	Plateaux pâtissiers rectangulaires à galerie	pièce		0.90	1.	1.10	1.25

			Nombre de places	4	6	8	12	18
168	Paniers à verres ordinaires	pièce			0.90	1.20	1.50	1.80
169	„ renforcés	„			1.20	1.60	2.	2.40
170	Paniers cuit-oeufs	„		0.25	0.35	0.40		

			Nombre de places	8	12	18	24
171	Buissons à oeufs pieds tissés	pièce		0.50	0.80	1.10	1.50

			Longueur	30	33	35	40	45 m
172	Fouets à oeufs manche fer à douille	douzaine		3.		4		
172 bis	„ „ „ extra forts	„		5.50	6.	6.50	7.25	9.50

Paniers spéciaux pour stérilisateurs, grenades incendie, etc... sur demande

162   163   164   167   165   170   168-169   171

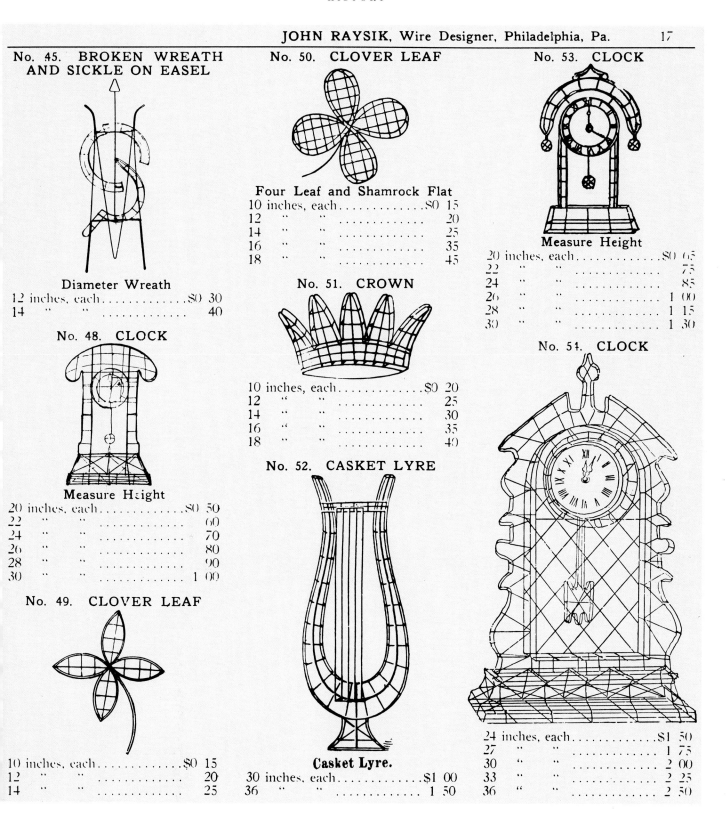

No. 45. BROKEN WREATH AND SICKLE ON EASEL

Diameter Wreath

12 inches, each	....	$0 30
14 " "	....	40

No. 48. CLOCK

Measure Height

20 inches, each	....	$0 50
22 " "	....	60
24 " "	....	70
26 " "	....	80
28 " "	....	90
30 " "	....	1 00

No. 49. CLOVER LEAF

10 inches, each	....	$0 15
12 " "	....	20
14 " "	....	25

No. 50. CLOVER LEAF

Four Leaf and Shamrock Flat

10 inches, each	....	$0 15
12 " "	....	20
14 " "	....	25
16 " "	....	35
18 " "	....	45

No. 51. CROWN

10 inches, each	....	$0 20
12 " "	....	25
14 " "	....	30
16 " "	....	35
18 " "	....	40

No. 52. CASKET LYRE

Casket Lyre.

30 inches, each	....	$1 00
36 " "	....	1 50

No. 53. CLOCK

Measure Height

20 inches, each	....	$0 65
22 " "	....	75
24 " "	....	85
26 " "	....	1 00
28 " "	....	1 15
30 " "	....	1 30

No. 54. CLOCK

24 inches, each	....	$1 50
27 " "	....	1 75
30 " "	....	2 00
33 " "	....	2 25
36 " "	....	2 50

16. Drahtbinder.

ABOVE Two tinkers, photographed in Vienna, 1878. Považské Museum, Žilina

RIGHT Pavol Sochan, an itinerant tinker photographed at the beginning of the twentieth century, came from the town of Trenčín, Slovakia, which was known for its numerous wire artisans. Slovak Ethnographic Museum, Martin

LEFT At the turn of the century Russia was an important destination for emigrating tinkers. There were about eighty workshops similar to this one, which belonged to Jozef Kolárik in St. Petersburg. Považské Museum, Žilina

BELOW Ján Vartál's workshop in New York at the beginning of the century produced wire armatures for lampshades. Považské Museum, Žilina

MASTERPIECES

At the Exposition of French Industrial Products that took place at the Louvre Palace in Paris in 1823, Henry Stammler, a manufacturer of stainless steel jewelry and wire objects from Strasbourg, exhibited some of his wares. He received a bronze medal in recognition of the workmanship of the objects he had crafted. Because these pieces had been made in what was still considered an ordinary material—especially as compared with the more inherently valuable silver and brass—it was the exceptional craftsmanship that allowed them to enter the realm of the decorative arts.

Once rudimentary, the technique of wirework had little by little brought forth a rivalry among its craftsmen, who had become more and more dexterous with the material and its creative possibilities. Crafting an important piece included forming the main armature with thick wire. Thinner wire was then woven over the armature, sometimes along with coiled wire for ornamentation. Extra decoration could be obtained by braiding different lengths of wire into garlands, tassels, and spirals and adding them on top of the armature. A date, a name, a monogram, or a heart could also be affixed, as if embroidered, to the most ambitious designs. The entire piece was then tinned, a procedure that assured solidity and retarded rusting. None of the elements was ever soldered, and every length of wire was bent and wound without heat. The most delicate of decorations were attached to the piece with the thinnest wire available.

By the beginning of the nineteenth century it was already a custom to commission exceptional pieces from wire craftsmen for important occasions, especially weddings. The objects would be displayed with pride in memory of the special event, becoming part of the family's patrimony. These trousseau baskets, fruit stands, candelabras, and chandeliers, already prized when they were created, were handed down from generation to generation. Unlike their more utilitarian counterparts, they were rarely subjected to daily use. Today they are extremely rare and considered chefs d'oeuvre not only of their time but of ours.

RIGHT A combination candelabra and plant stand. This extravagant design, dripping with small cone-shaped tassels and loaded with ribbons and curlicues of wire, was inspired by the decorative excesses of the French Second Empire style.

ABOVE A hanging planter decorated with thick tassels of twisted wire and four tightly woven chains.

ABOVE AND RIGHT A surprising hanging basket with cover, made as part of a trousseau. It was probably hung in a prominent place in the house so that it could be admired. The detail exhibits the technical prowess of the maker, who kept his patterns secret.

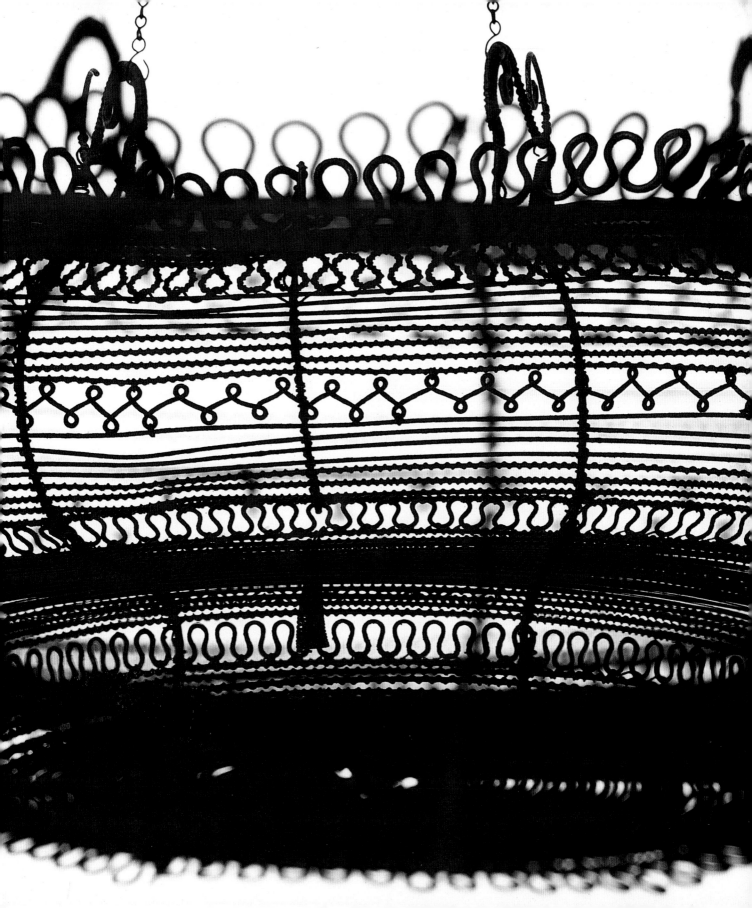

ABOVE Extravagantly detailed baskets were often examples of a craftsman's dexterity and were more decorative than utilitarian. Especially in the rural areas, the largest ones were traditionally made to hold linens and other precious items of a young bride's trousseau.

RIGHT On this stylish painted sconce, probably dating from the 1930s, wire has been rolled into a series of flat coils.

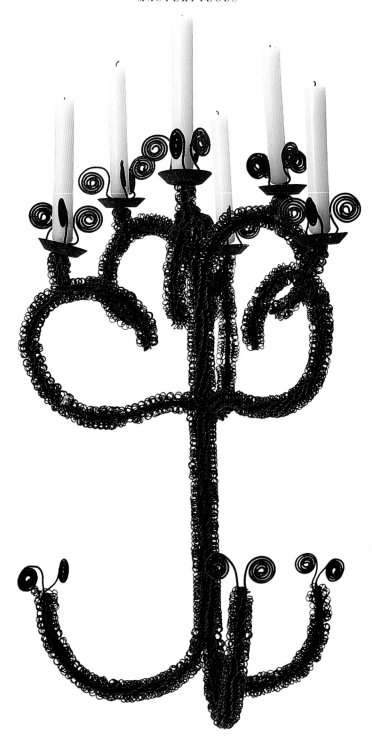

A standing candelabra for six candles has a rusticated look. Its elegant
shape contrasts with its rather rudimentary workmanship. The only
purely fanciful elements are the coils that secure the candles and finish
off the three legs of the pedestal.

Impressive yet delicate, this eight-branch candelabra was a one-of-a-kind decorative design that rivaled its heavier brass and wrought-iron counterparts.

THE TABLE

By the end of the nineteenth century the setting of an elegant table was already a well-honed practice among the wealthy bourgeoisie. The large dining room with its imposing mahogany table and suite of matching chairs was proof that one belonged to the middle class.

The Industrial Revolution ensured the availability of new wares manufactured at lower prices, and the *art de vivre*—with all of its new conventions—reached a whole new stratum of society. These new status seekers were eager to furnish their homes with extensive and elaborate dinner sets, even if most of the dishes were rarely used.

Formal entertaining—with a vast array of dishes—necessitated extensive advance planning on the part of both the hostess and the guests, who assiduously consulted the popular etiquette manuals in order not to be caught off guard during formal dinners, when simply reaching for the wrong fork could spell social disaster.

Huge dressers and buffets were the repositories of these treasures. The house was also filled up little by little with all kinds of bibelots and knickknacks bought during shopping trips to the new department stores or on travels abroad.

Wire objects were an important part of this fashionably cluttered decorative style. Now that wire was being manufactured industrially for the first time, it appeared in many different guises: it was married to majolica, made into tassel-bedecked platters, and wrought into fanciful baskets for displaying fruit and candies on the sideboard.

Different wire techniques emerged and resulted in a variety of decorative expressions. While some of the fanciful baskets and cake stands that were made in the 1870s of tinned twisted wire were based on French designs, many were made by craftsmen in small workshops, who often created their own variations.

Wire was also ideally suited to the kind of object that appealed to the gadget-minded. A folding and "convertible" wire basket made of nickeled iron wire was described in an early twentieth-century catalog as a "lamp shade, flower stand, egg boiler, hanging lamp, ladies' work basket, iron stand, card holder, cake stand, fruit basket, etc." Who could ask for anything more?

RIGHT A collection of wire-framed plates that were often used on the table to serve grapes now decorates the wall of a dining room.

Plates, some of majolica by Hippolyte Boulanger and some of Rubelles porcelain, others of earthenware manufactured at the end of the nineteenth century by Gien, Sarguemines, and Villeroy-Boch, and still others, more ordinary, of American pressed glass and cardboard chromolithographs that imitated crockery, were the base for a variety of wirework.

PRECEDING PAGES Majolica trivets edged with wire, as well as an extraordinary platter that, with its intricate design, tassels, and monogram, could easily rival its silver-plated counterparts.

ABOVE Baskets were popular containers and proved useful for holding floral centerpieces, fruit, bread, and pastries.

While some baskets were made as part of a series, others were crafted as
unique examples, customized with monograms and special decorations.

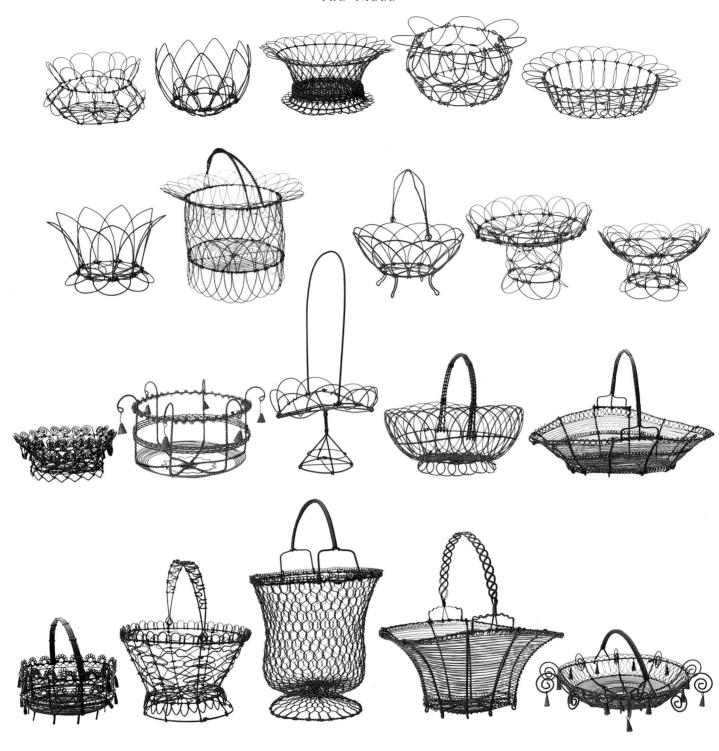

ABOVE Baskets of wire netting or braided wire, with and without handles, made into convertible and folding containers, show the imagination of the wireworker.

RIGHT A graceful fruit basket stands on a ceramic-tiled stove.

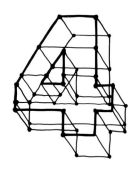

THE KITCHEN

In the old days the kitchen was truly the heart of the home. Centered around the fireplace, the country kitchen was not only where the family came together for meals but where sewing and weaving took place, where food was cooked and preserved, and where such necessities as candles and baskets were made.

The introduction of the freestanding coal or wood-burning stove at the beginning of the nineteenth century not only changed the organization of the kitchen but also influenced cooking methods. Tinning, which became commonplace at the time, made the new brass, iron, and wire utensils easier to use and maintain.

In most households, in the city as well as in the more rural areas, food preparation required a dizzying variety of utensils, from pots, molds, scales, squeezers, rolling pins, slicers, tongs, and kettles to dozens of graters, colanders, mashers, skimmers, ladles, tongs, and trivets, many of which were made of wire.

The new department stores fostered consumerism in the booming middle class, while the popular home-making books and cookbooks of the era also encouraged the use of a profusion of newfangled gadgets.

A 1905 catalog from Le Printemps, the Parisian department store, suggested *batteries de cuisine,* or sets of kitchen equipment, to suit a range of budgets. The smallest number of items deemed necessary was 106. The price rose with the quality. It was assumed that these utensils would serve a family for life, and the woman of the house—or her staff—was in charge of taking care of them.

The advent of electricity and with it the revolution in kitchen design and equipment reached its apotheosis in the streamlined American kitchen of the 1950s. Today we tend to look to the kitchens of the past with a more nostalgic eye, and many pieces of wire kitchenware, such as salad baskets, eggbeaters, potato mashers, and cake racks, still evoke the old-fashioned charm that characterized the kitchens we remember with so much affection.

RIGHT In the kitchen of an eighteenth-century house in the south of France, a group of wire kitchen utensils, including snail and salad baskets, teapot stands, and cake platters, is displayed on a painted antique buffet.

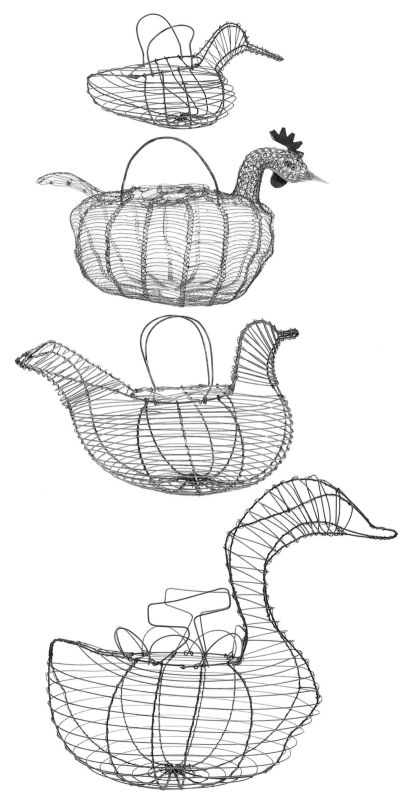

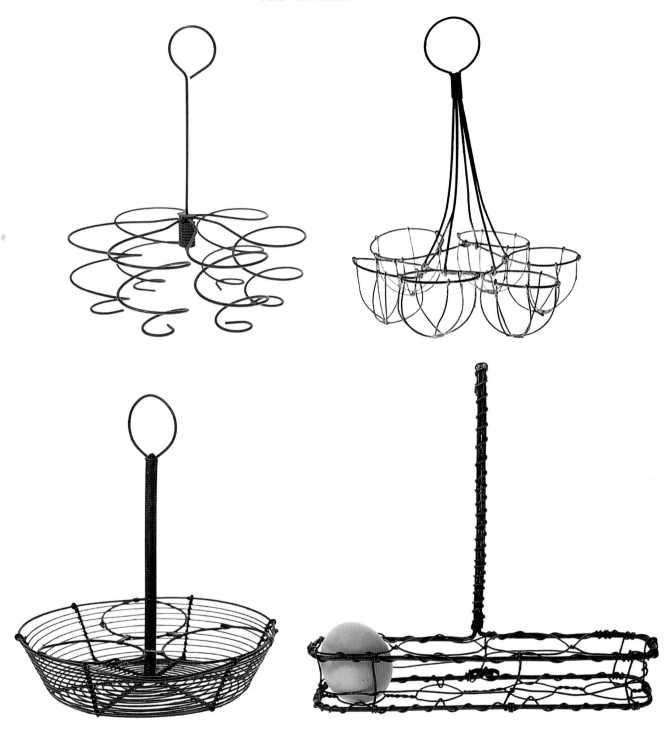

LEFT For centuries the egg has been the symbol of the farmyard. Newly laid eggs were a kitchen staple, whether scrambled, poached, boiled, whisked into sauces, or made into pastry dough. There were wire utensils for every application. It all began with gathering the eggs from the henhouse and carrying them home in chicken- or duck-shaped baskets.

ABOVE Long-handled wire baskets and racks were used especially for submerging eggs in hot water to poach or boil them. There were models for cooking up to twelve eggs at a time.

A traditional presence on zinc counters in French cafés and brasseries,
standing egg trees held the hard-boiled eggs that served as a snack
accompanied by a pinch of salt and a buttered baguette.

Vintage catalogs illustrated egg trees that were available for six, twelve, or twenty-four eggs and were sometimes used in the home. The small basket at the top was for the salt cellar.

The beating and whisking of eggs—both yolks and whites—gave rise to
a multitude of whisks, many of which were patented in the second half
of the nineteenth century.

Whisks and whips, ideal for incorporating egg yolks into mayonnaise,
were popular inventions of the day. The one in the middle was even
equipped with its own oil reservoir.

ABOVE In France, eating fresh lettuce has been customary since the end of the eighteenth century. Baskets to wash the lettuce in were made from wire that was twisted and curled to imitate the graceful shapes of the older rattan baskets.

RIGHT The salad spinner, with its rotating system to remove excess water, was a late nineteenth-century invention that is still made today in colored plastic.

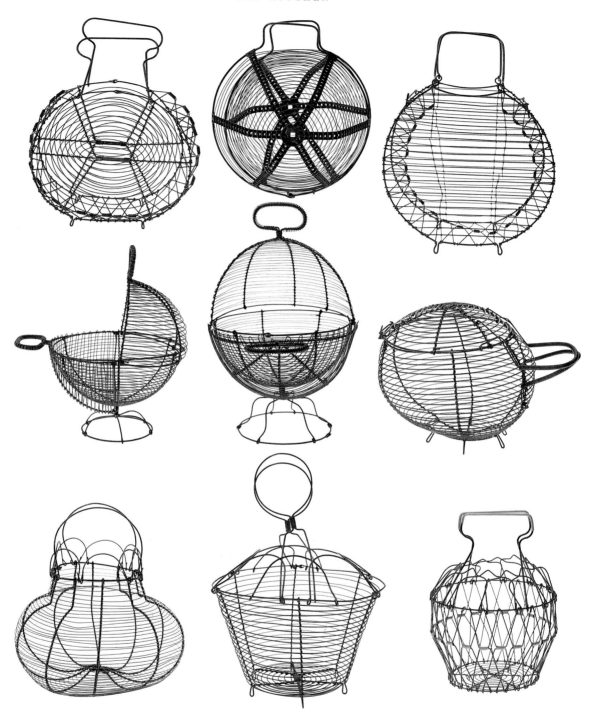

ABOVE AND RIGHT By the beginning of the nineteenth century salad dryers were indispensable in every kitchen. Numerous shapes were available. Some could be folded, some came with covers. From the early nineteenth century on, many manuals advised wiping the metal baskets dry after every use to prevent them from rusting.

OVERLEAF Sometimes craftsmen would make salad baskets to mark special occasions such as weddings. The date or monogram was "embroidered" in wire.

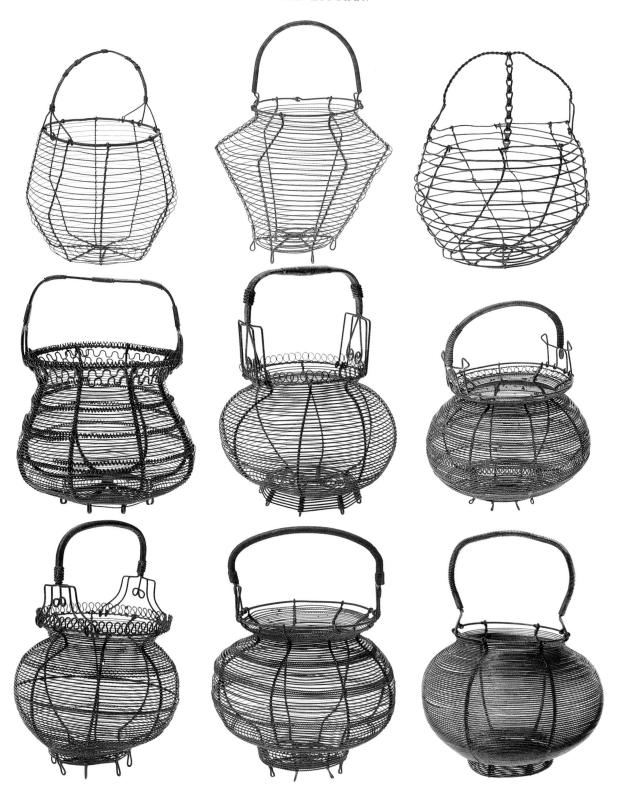

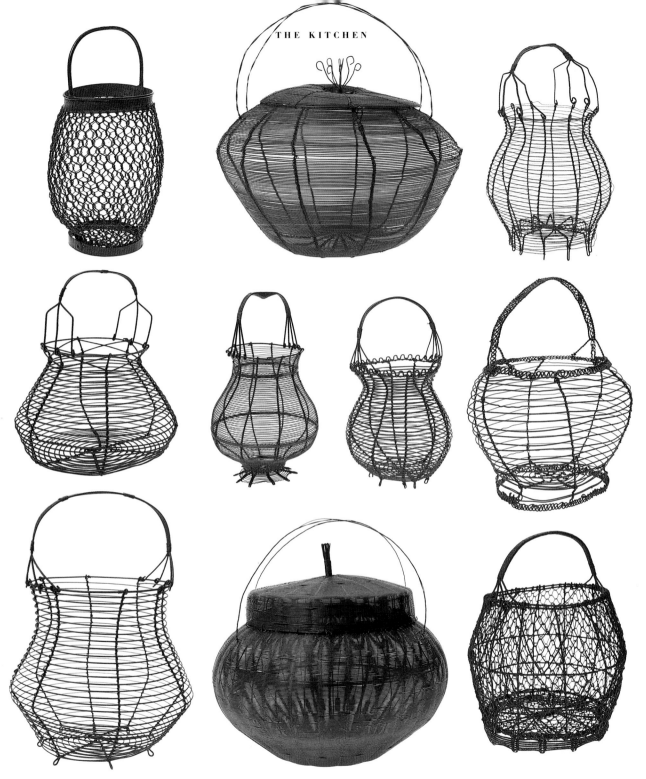

Although similar in shape and often confused with salad baskets, snail baskets tended to be larger and more elongated and usually had narrower necks. When they had covers, the baskets were also used to purge, or clean, the snails with flour before cooking.

Cooking on an open hearth was the norm—especially in the country-
side—until the stove became standard equipment. Bread was toasted
in a variety of grills. In France thick slices of country bread were toasted

vertically in front of the fire (**LEFT**), while in the United States thin slices of bread were held directly over the flames in a horizontal position (**ABOVE**).

Larger, double-sided griddles were used to cook and barbecue meat and
fish either in the hearth or outdoors.

PRECEDING PAGES Decorative wall-hung racks are still used today to display folk-art objects and wire kitchen utensils.

ABOVE LEFT A crocheted cotton basket suspended from a wire ring was used to store onions in the kitchen.

ABOVE RIGHT Of a similar design, the spoon holder was a common utensil in Central European country kitchens.

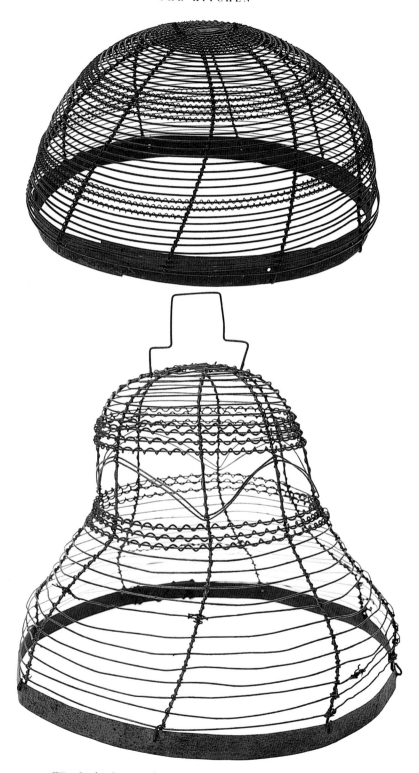

Wire food safes were for protecting just-prepared dishes from household pets.

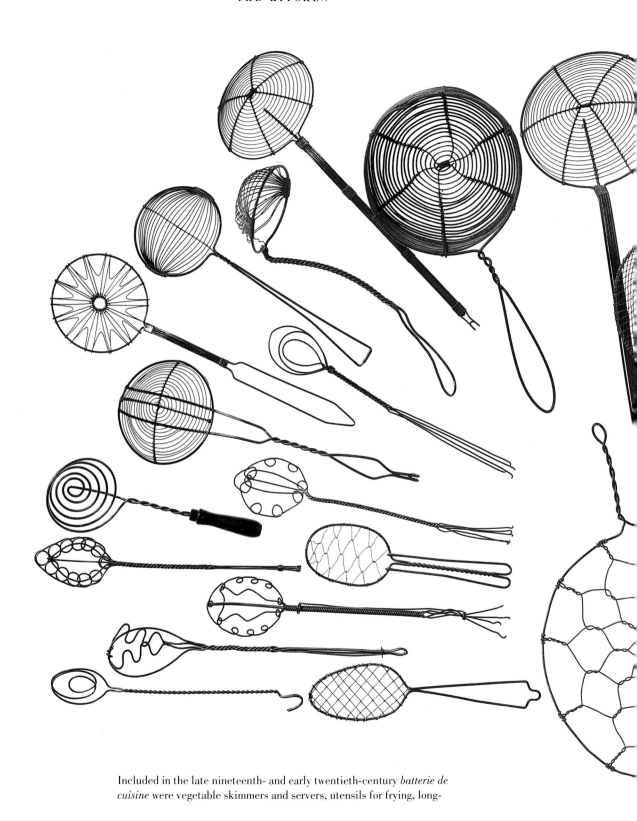

Included in the late nineteenth- and early twentieth-century *batterie de cuisine* were vegetable skimmers and servers, utensils for frying, long-

handled forks for grilling over a flame, Swedish dough perforators, potato mashers, and combination whisk and dishcloth grapples.

Wire racks, usually round or rectangular in shape and available in many
different sizes, were used for cooling candies, cakes, and cookies.

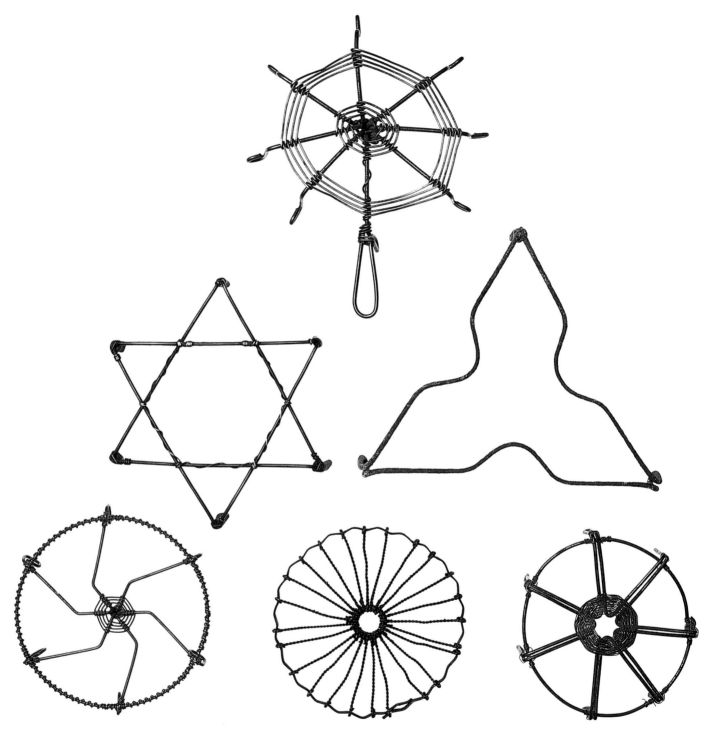

ABOVE AND RIGHT Teapot and coffeepot stands, trivets, and other pot stands were designed in fanciful shapes and often roughly crafted. Made of twisted tinned wire or coiled wire, some were mass-produced by small manufacturers and others were individually crafted.

OVERLEAF LEFT A rack that could hold different-sized pot lids was a convenient kitchen accessory.

OVERLEAF RIGHT Many old butcher shops had special wire racks to hold sausages and white and black puddings.

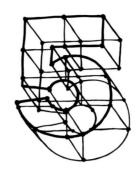

THE WINE CELLAR

In France, whether in Burgundy or in the Bordeaux region, in Alsace or along the Rhone Valley, the production of great wines involves a savoir faire that has been handed down from generation to generation. Vineyards are considered to be man-sized when the family—father and son especially—is able to work the five-hectare plot with very little outside help.

In the multistep process of winemaking, wire first appeared in the various filters that helped separate the residue from the pressed grapes. Wire was also fashioned into elaborate bottle holders that were deemed elegant enough to be brought to the dinner table. Wire glass carriers and egg holders were regulars on the old-fashioned zinc counters of most cafés, especially the small neighborhood bistros called *bougnats* that until about twenty years ago were typical Parisian fixtures, where it was possible to buy wood and coal along with the just-arrived Beaujolais Nouveau.

Wine in barrels was sold to *négociants,* or merchants, who stocked their vintages in large warehouses or cellars before bottling and selling them to restaurants, bistros and wine shops. The cool cellar was where wine was tasted, judged, and appreciated. It was there that good wines, with the help of time, attained their noble stature.

Going down to the cellar to choose a bottle of wine was a daily activity. What could have been more convenient in the days before electricity than to have a bottle carrier equipped with a candleholder to light the way?

Winemaking was a way of life governed by distinctive rhythms and requiring a variety of tools and utensils that were used at different points in the process culminating in the myriad corkscrews without which wine tasting would be far less ceremonial.

With the exception of corkscrews, wire objects that are connected to winemaking are typically and exclusively French. Their specificity and rarity have made them much in demand by international antiques dealers and collectors for whom the culture and history of wine has become a new passion.

RIGHT A French wine caddy in the shape of a chariot; its wheels allow the wine to be served without removing the bottle from its holder. The shape of the Second Empire–style holder was copied from the distinctive bottle of Burgundy.

Wire wine caddies, from the simplest to the most rococo designs, were widely used at home and in restaurants until the first decades of this century. It was recommended, especially for older wines, to place uncorked bottles at a slight angle for a few hours to allow any sediment to settle.

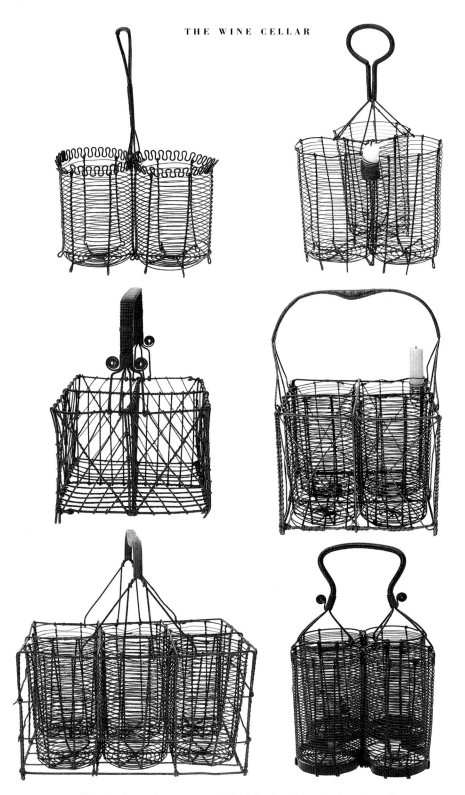

Wire bottle carriers were useful both for fetching wine from the cellar
and for bringing it home from the wine merchant. Carriers accommodat-
ing four or six bottles were reinforced with an extra wire armature.

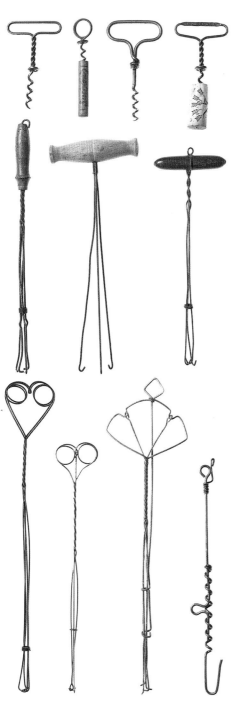

ABOVE Of the thousands of corkscrews that exist, a handful are made entirely of wire. Wire was also useful in making cork retrievers.

RIGHT Wire glass carriers have proven to be as practical as they are decorative.

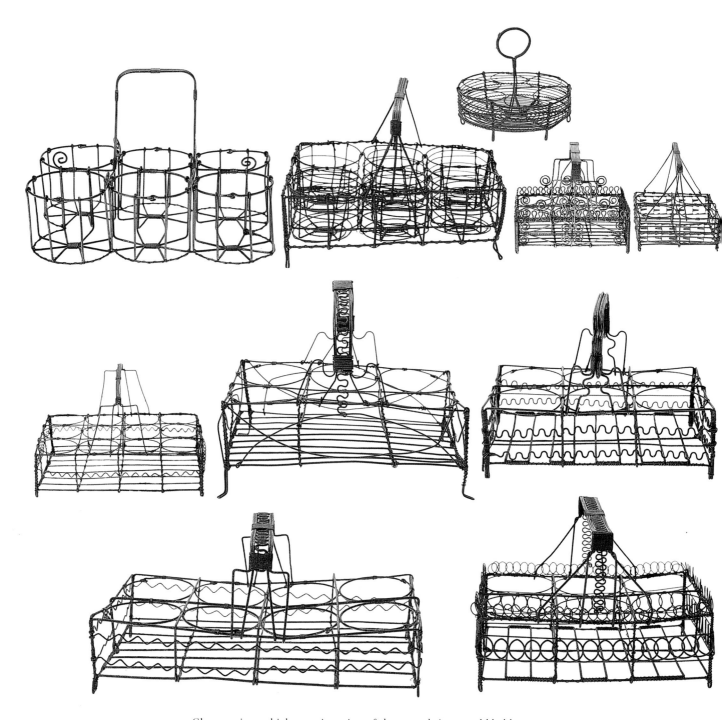

Glass carriers, which came in variety of shapes and sizes, could hold up to a dozen glasses and tumblers. In French cafés they were kept within easy reach on the counter. They proved particularly useful in Provence for carrying out the traditional pastis to people playing pétanque on the square.

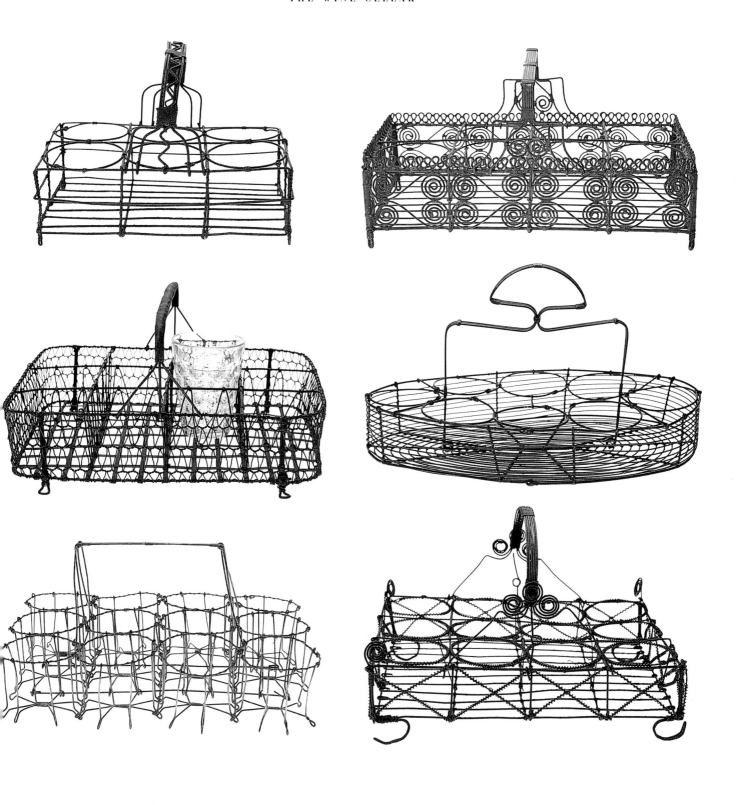

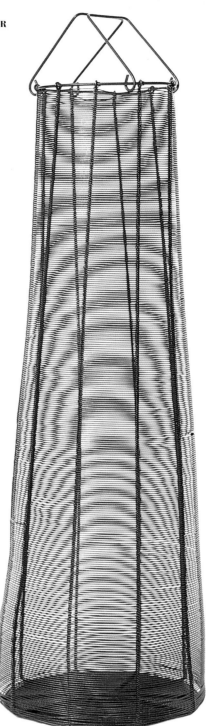

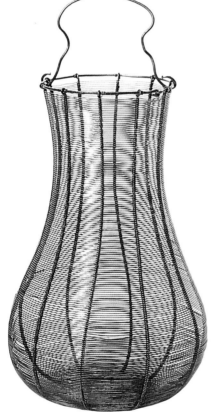

TOP A barrel strainer placed on the tap of the vat separated the thin grape skins and stalks from the juice during tunning.

ABOVE AND ABOVE RIGHT Tall wire filters were used to separate the juice of the crushed grapes from the pips and skins.

RIGHT Traditionally, in France one tasted a wine after having eaten a walnut. In an old wine cellar a rare wrought-iron wine-tasting stand that includes a wire nut basket is positioned near an unusual bottle carrier in the shape of a pyramid. Because of the horizontal position of the bottles, the carrier can also be used as a wine rack.

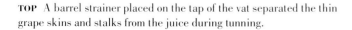

HOUSEKEEPING

Throughout the nineteenth century and well into the twentieth, especially before labor- and time-saving devices took some of the drudgery out of running a household, housekeeping was exclusively the woman's domain. From early morning to night, and almost every day of the year, housekeeping tasks were repeated according to an established rhythm, whether in modest country homes or in wealthier households with a battery of servants. Each one necessitated a particular ability that was passed down from grandmother to mother to daughter.

Homemaking books abounded, and toward the end of the nineteenth century mail-order catalogs offered a wide selection of tempting new products. While many of these objects became standard equipment in the home, some were crafted as unique pieces, exceptional for the creativity and skill of the individual artisan who made them.

Throughout the nineteenth century wire objects served as ingenious accessories to housekeeping tasks from drying linens and safely holding hot irons to beating pillows and carpets. There were wire racks for drip-drying dishes; wall-hung racks for the ubiquitous dishcloths; embellished holders for sponges and soap; a variety of iron stands, each with a distinctive motif, pincushions that were part of the well-stocked sewing basket; and a multitude of carpet and pillow beaters in which wire was bent, looped, and braided according to the imagination of the maker.

Other amenities of the home, such as lighting and heating, were also sources for wire inventions. There were candle holders that lighted trips to the cellar and wire guards that protected early lightbulbs. Fancifully decorated wire screens covered the fireplace, protecting floors and carpets from hot embers.

Although some of these once useful objects have disappeared, replaced by modern appliances and utensils —from automatic clothes dryers to vacuum cleaners— some still retain their original function. Even in houses where the fireplace is no longer the only source of heat, a wire firescreen can add to the coziness and safety of sitting near the hearth.

Other items—inventive wire hangers, for example— are today sought out by collectors. Appreciated for their graphic qualities, they are now displayed on the wall instead of lined up in the closet.

RIGHT A mid-nineteenth-century pincushion, its blue-covered pillow stuffed with cotton or wool and its elaborate wire stand adorned with flower-shaped pendants, was the pride of a sewing basket.

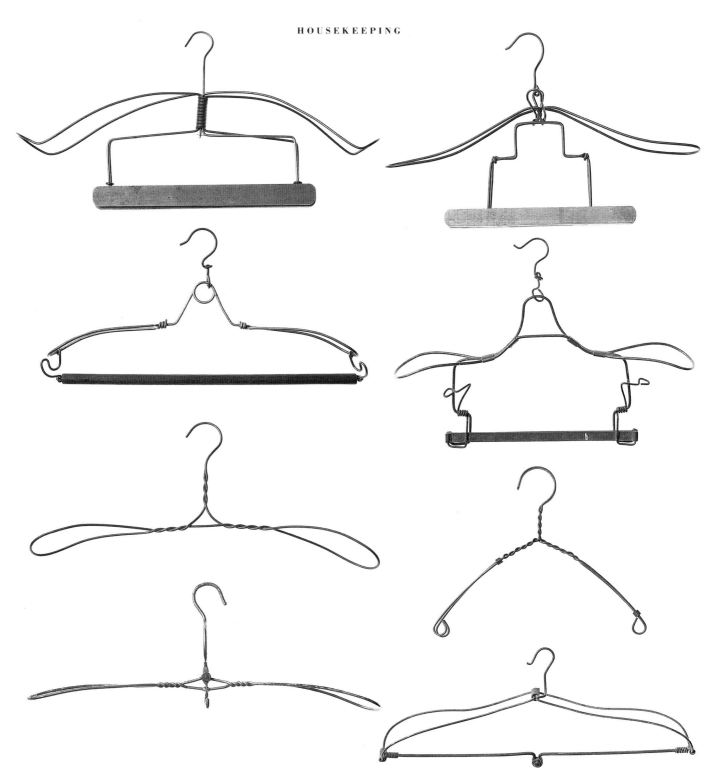

Hangers, wrought from steel wire and either tinned, nickel-plated, or painted, were made in a wide variety of shapes at the turn of the century. Available from numerous catalogs and small companies, many had their own patent numbers. They were used in the home as well as on the road to hold or dry the specific garments for which they were designed. Some folded ingeniously; others were equipped to hold pants or skirts. Still others, like those at the far right, had steel wire twisted into springy coils to provide padded support for more delicate pieces of clothing.

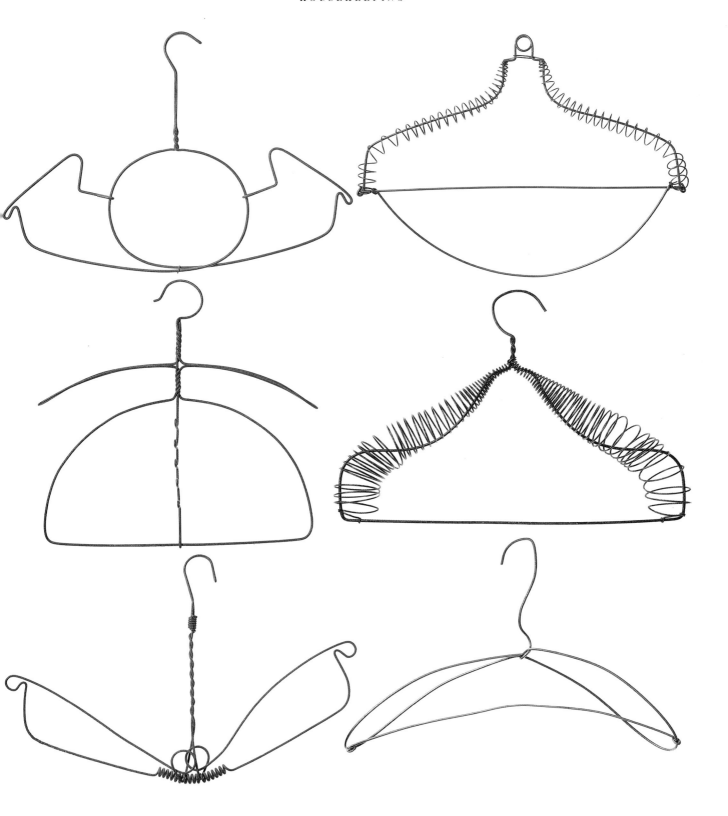

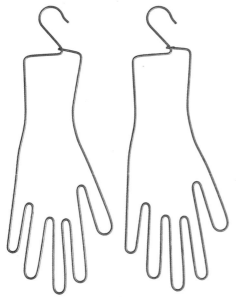

ABOVE Wire forms were used for drying rubber kitchen gloves or to keep kid and fabric gloves from losing their shape if they got wet. Similar forms existed for socks and stockings.

RIGHT Especially in inclement weather, clothes were often dried near the fireplace or stove. Some drying racks used to hang from the ceiling; others were freestanding and folding. A wall-hung rack with folding arms was a clever early twentieth-century invention that was as practical as it was space-saving.

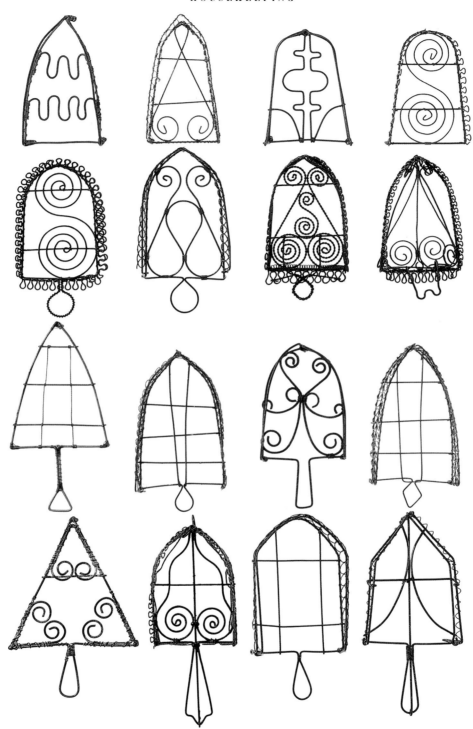

Ironing was an important and time-consuming household task. A number of flatirons and sadirons—as solid, heavy irons were called—were heated on the stove at the same time. A variety of trivets and stands made of wire, as shown here, and also of brass, cut-out sheet iron, and cast iron, were on hand when the ironer needed to pause or change irons. Some had looped handles so that they could be hung on the wall when not in use.

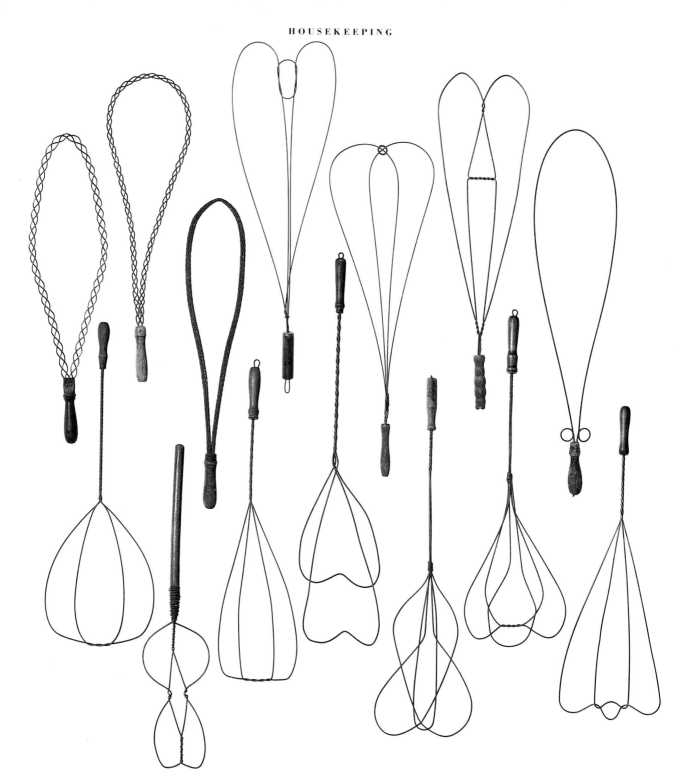

ABOVE AND RIGHT Before carpet sweepers and electric vacuum cleaners made their appearance, housewives were bombarded with catalogs filled with a multitude of rug and carpet beaters. Every new design, accompanied by such catchy slogans as "beat but can't be beaten," was meant to make the outdoor task of getting rid of dust more efficient. Wire beaters were the American counterpart of the rattan beaters more common in Europe.

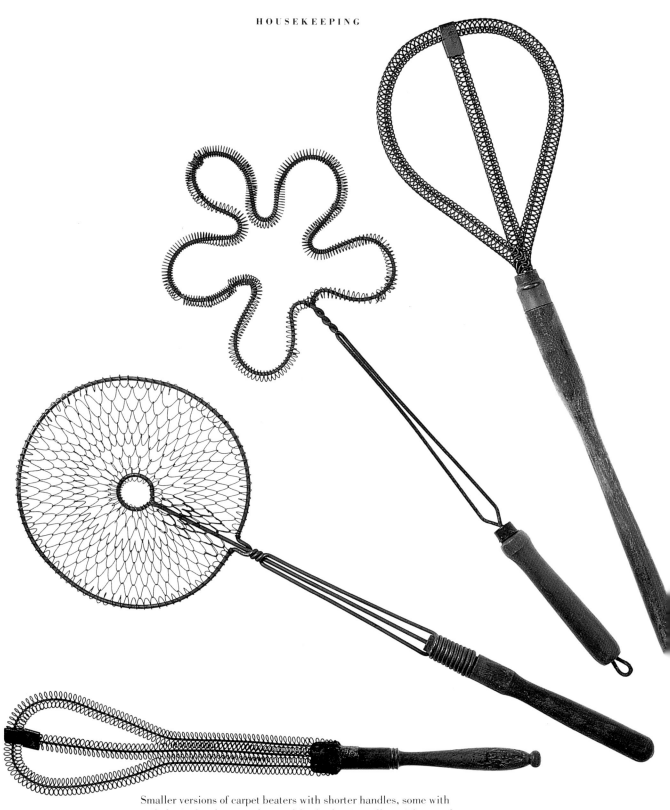

Smaller versions of carpet beaters with shorter handles, some with coiled-wire heads, were also used for freshening pillows. The metal was often galvanized to avoid rust stains.

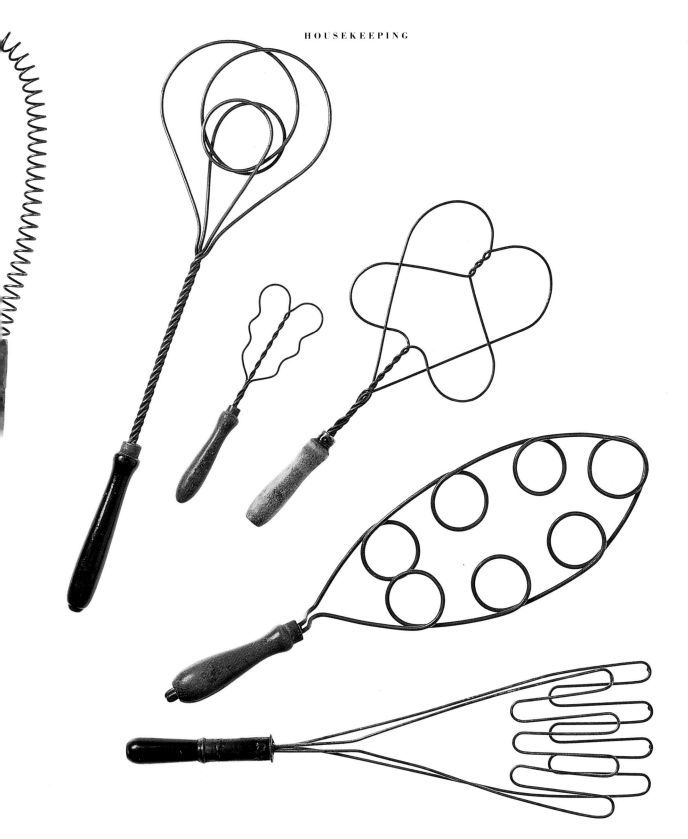

Soap holders, sponge baskets, and toilet-paper holders were fashioned out of wire and hung near tubs, sinks, and toilets. Soap was a rarity in ordinary households until the 1880s, when it began to be produced in large blocks for laundry and bathing. Natural sponges were used instead of washcloths, and they were placed in the wire holders to dry. In an 1888 catalog a toilet-paper holder called a closet paper rack, large enough to accommodate sheets or rolls of paper, was already being offered.

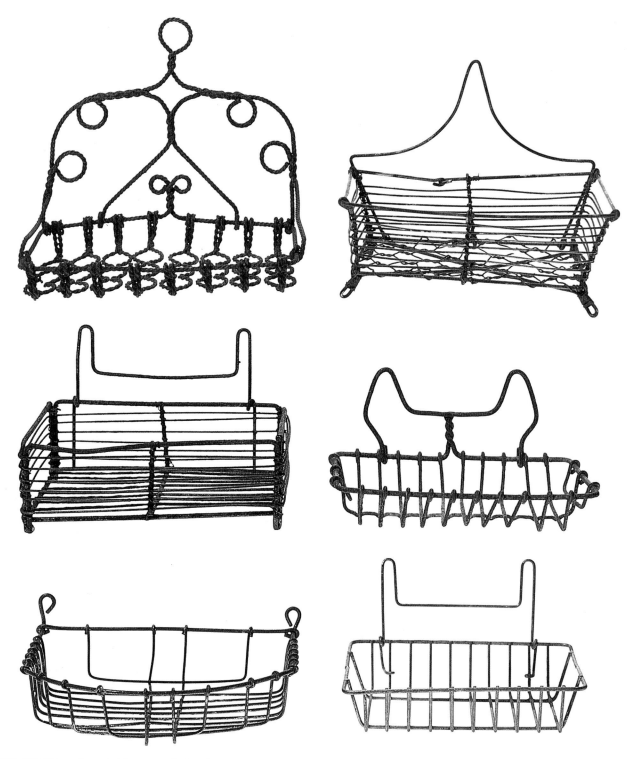

ABOVE AND RIGHT Some holders were designed to accommodate tooth-brushes and nail brushes as well as tumblers.

OVERLEAF Drying racks for dishes were placed close to the sink, even before running water was commonplace. Pot-chain brushes, with and without handles, were used for scrubbing pots.

ABOVE Wall-hung racks of different sizes held dishcloths as well as kitchen utensils.

RIGHT Coiled-wire candlestick sockets could be adjusted up and down. The big handle was for carrying or hanging the candle holders, which were usually used for trips to the cellar.

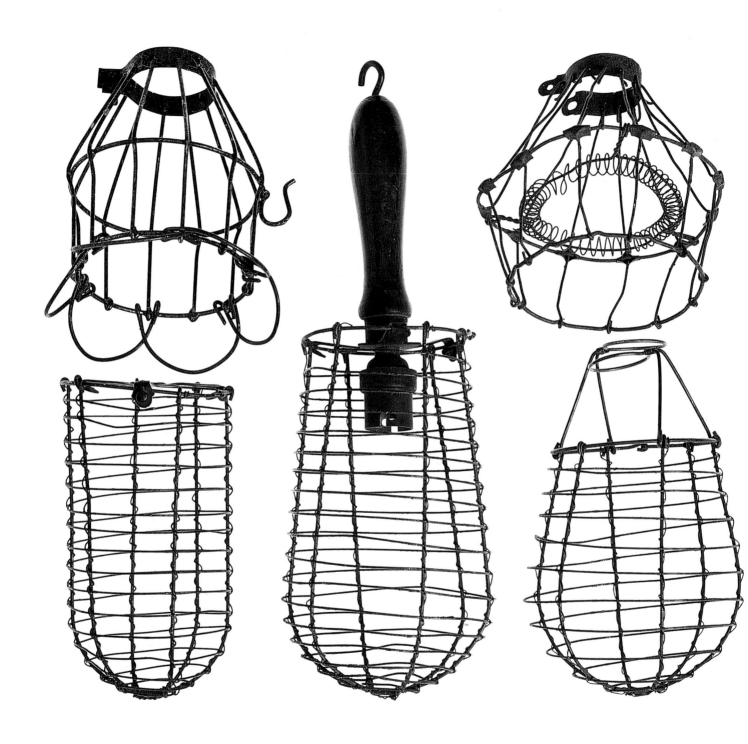

When electricity was installed at the beginning of the century, wire
guards were used to protect lightbulbs from shattering. Some had hooks
so that they could be hung in cellars and at construction sites.

Oil lamps, typically used by shepherds in their shelters in the Alps, have glass reservoirs, cotton wicks, and wire harps for carrying and hanging.

LEFT The fireplace was the center of the house, especially in the winter months when a slow-burning fire was always maintained. At night screens were placed in front of the smoldering logs to protect floors and furnishings from embers.

ABOVE At the turn of the century new fire extinguishers were patented. In case of an out-of-control fire, glass bottles, stored in wire holders, were thrown onto the flames. The shattered bottles released a gas that put out the fire.

THE GARDEN

The relationship between house and garden has long been sympathetic. A hundred years ago the wide porch, the long veranda, and the new industrially made glassed-in conservatory were in fashion, satisfying the Victorians' predilection for nature, sometimes without even requiring one to leave the house.

Indoors, in plush parlors and dining rooms, plants—especially those that did not need too much natural light—were displayed in tall jardinieres, huge majolica pots often raised on pedestals, and tiered étagères. For the first time, overscale cast-iron vases and urns decorated with classical motifs and friezes were produced in hundreds of styles in small factories all over the United States. Wire was ideally suited for plant stands, graceful hanging baskets, all kinds of whatnots, and a variety of topiary forms—the geometric or animal shapes that were popular decorations in many gardens.

Many of the large topiary forms that resurface today in antiques stores and garden shops and are sold as "sculptural" forms were in fact crafted for professiona florists who specialized in funerary bouquets and could use the various shapes over and over again, hiding thei armature with fresh blooms. Artisans who came from Slovakia and settled near Philadelphia and Chicago a the turn of the century were the ones who brought thi traditional wirework technique to America.

Bird cages also provided a good excuse for flights o fancy in wire. Inspired by many architectural styles from the Gothic church to the Oriental palace, they could be small enough to house a single canary or large enough to accommodate a flock of doves. Wire was a particularly good material for these airy and transparent architectural abodes.

Cut flowers were a new luxury in the Victorian age especially in the growing urban centers. In Europe as well as America ambitious arrangements of fresh flowers were a sure sign of wealth and taste. It is not surprising that numerous wire "frogs"—which remained silent and invisible—were devised to hold flowers securely in tall or short vases.

RIGHT A topiary form in the shape of a child's chair is an American design from the first decades of the century. It now hangs on a garden wall so that its sculptural shape can be appreciated.

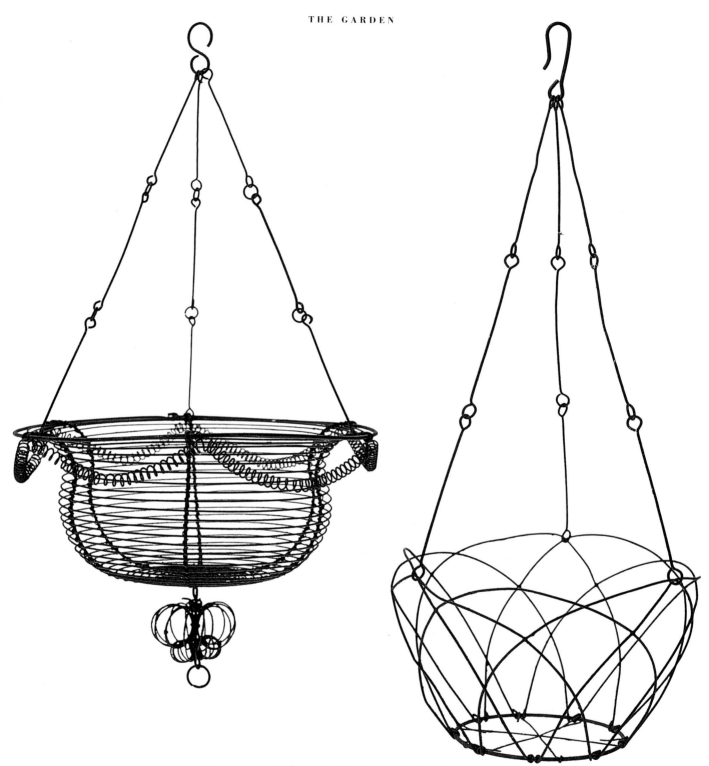

ABOVE AND RIGHT Delicate hanging planters lined with moss were
suspended along verandas or in front of windows. They could hold small
flowerpots. The planter shown above right is American; the other two
are French.

ABOVE This three-tiered display rack was probably a countertop shop fitting in which miniature plants were offered for sale.

RIGHT Two elegant parrot-shaped topiary forms perch atop a stone garden sculpture depicting an arrangement of fruits and flowers.

A selection of the wire forms executed in the traditional way by Slovakian immigrants in America includes a six-foot-high heart and various Masonic emblems. The forms, covered with fresh flowers, were presented at funerals and burials. They tended to reflect the departed's profession or illustrate a particular sentiment that family, friends, or colleagues wished to convey.

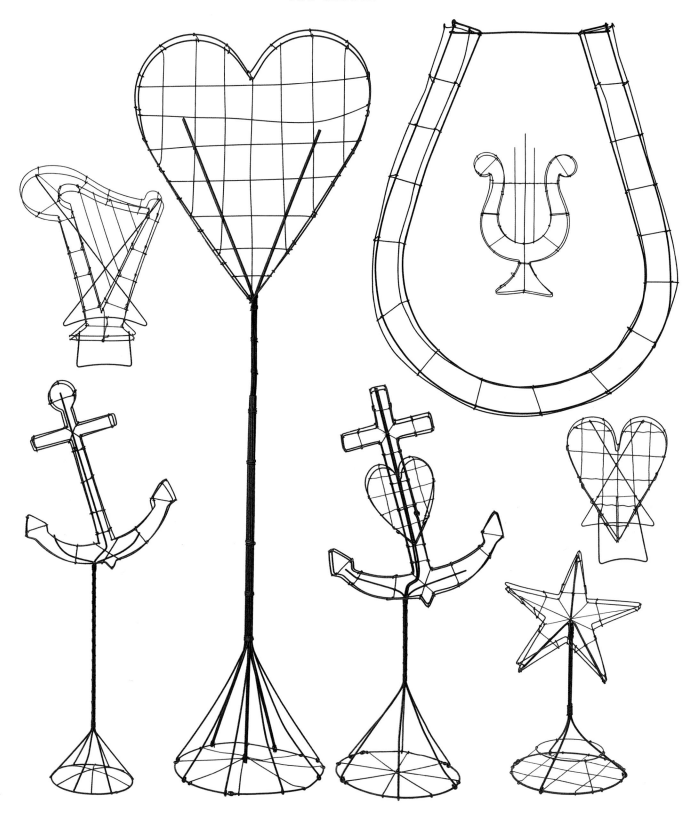

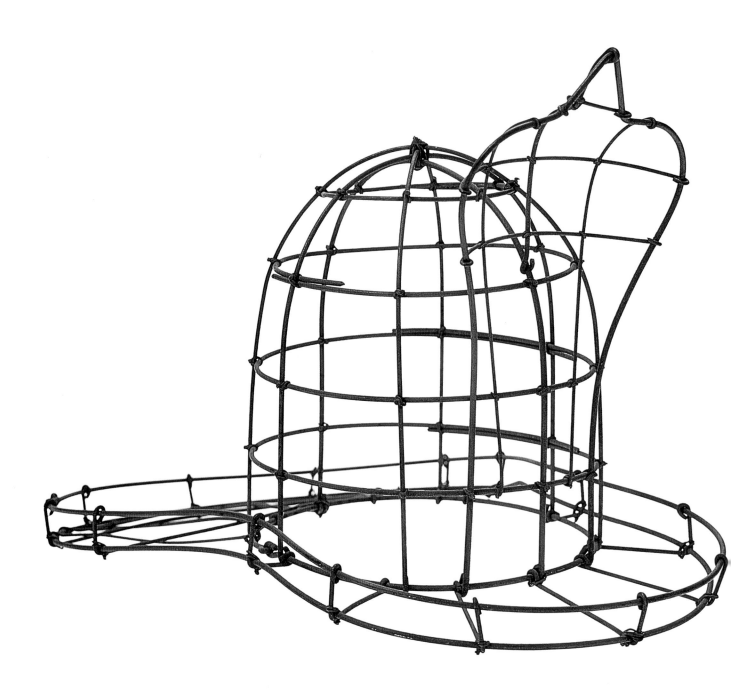

ABOVE This wire form in the shape of an American turn-of-the-century fireman's helmet would have been covered in flowers to mark the death of a fireman who may have succumbed in the line of duty.

RIGHT An English garden planter, originally part of the furnishings of a Victorian conservatory. Many versions of this kind of planter were available a hundred years ago. Often they were painted to protect them from rust.

Architectural bird cages were crafted for housing birds indoors in high style. Parrots, parakeets, and canaries were prized pets and were often kept in large domed or turreted cages.

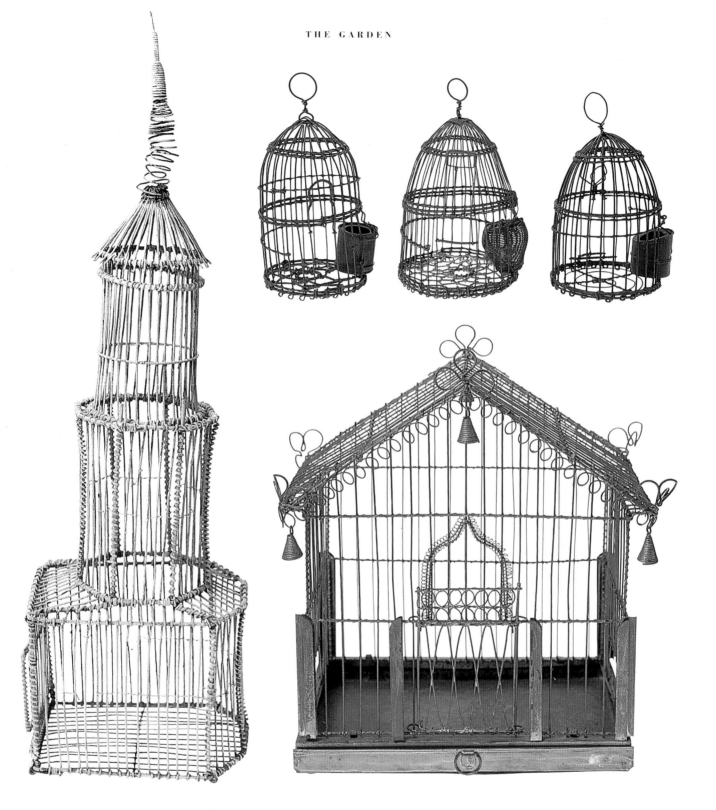

The three small cages were for carrying small birds home from
the market.

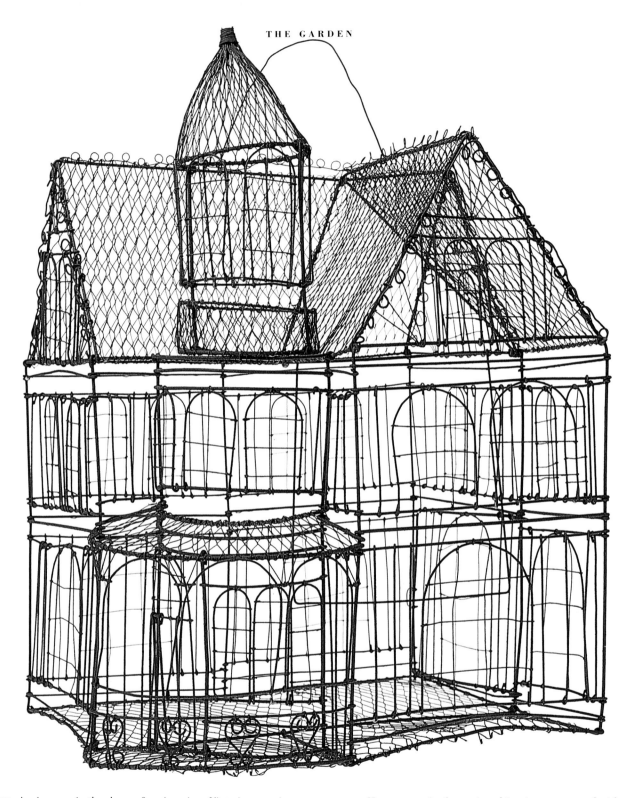

THE GARDEN

ABOVE A wire cage in the shape of an American Victorian mansion looks like a birdhouse but was never used as one. It was probably crafted for a window display at the end of the nineteenth century.

RIGHT Home to a pair of canaries, this wire cage topped with a sunrise motif hangs on the shutters of a house in southwest France.

Thick wire used to be coiled and twisted into flower holders that were
readily adaptable to all different kinds of flowers and arrangements.
Nowadays these frogs are collected more for their eccentric sculptural
shapes than for their original function.

GENERAL STORE

In America the general or country store came into its own in the last half of the nineteenth century. As the railroad extended westward and people returning from the Civil War looked for new commercial endeavors, stores that offered a wide range of goods proliferated in every town or outpost. Peddlers who had traveled far selling the wares they carried on their backs or on pushcarts now set up shop and became more established merchants. A barter system, allowing locally made or cultivated goods to be exchanged for manufactured products, helped the economic development of the area.

The general store was the center of the community, the place where news and gossip were exchanged, where products were on display, and where people often congregated around the wood-burning stove to discuss politics, the weather, and what was happening on the farm across the valley. Eventually the growing mail-order business somewhat threatened the commercial success of the general store, if not its appeal as a social center.

As the name suggests, one could find everything one needed or wanted in general stores, which were known as bazaars in Europe. Outside the large cities the general store was usually the only place to shop for groceries, hardware, and housewares, as well as the newest fashions and gadgets.

Wire items abounded. Some, like colanders and ladles, were the traditional wares of the tinker or peddler; others, including fishing paraphernalia, were manufactured by the small specialized workshops that developed in the second half of the nineteenth century. Some wire items were for sale, while others were part of the display and furnishings of the stores themselves. Postcards, which were in their heyday at the turn of the century, were displayed on revolving wire racks; brown paper bags in which customers would put their purchases were available in a range of sizes and stored neatly in standing wire racks; and the latest fashions were draped on graceful wire mannequins.

Today supermarkets and discount chains have replaced the general store. The everyday products that once filled the cluttered counters and bustling aisles of the general store have now joined the ranks of memorabilia that are as rare as they are filled with nostalgia.

RIGHT Vintage postcards are displayed in a revolving wire rack in front of a seed cabinet in a French shop.

ABOVE Postcard holders in the shape of fans, wall-hung or freestanding, were popular for displaying keepsakes.

RIGHT A wall-mounted wire rack was used to hold newspapers.

Wire wastebaskets were a staple of offices. Some were placed under oak desks, others were hung on the wall. Many models were stocked in the general store or available by mail order.

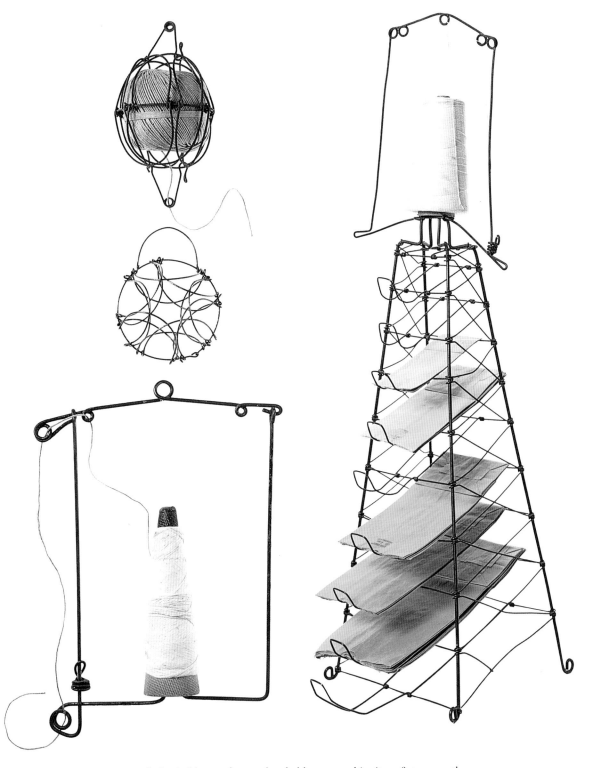

String holders and paper-bag holders were ubiquitous fixtures on the
counters of general stores.

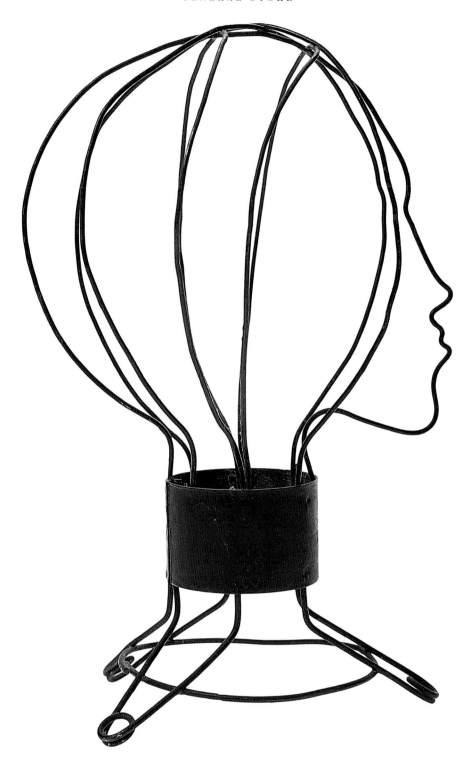

Wire shaped in the form of a head was used to display hats in a
1940s shop.

One can still imagine the sailor suit and wedding dress that must have been displayed on these two 1860s mannequins, one in the shape of a young boy, the other fitted with a wasp waist and flared skirt.

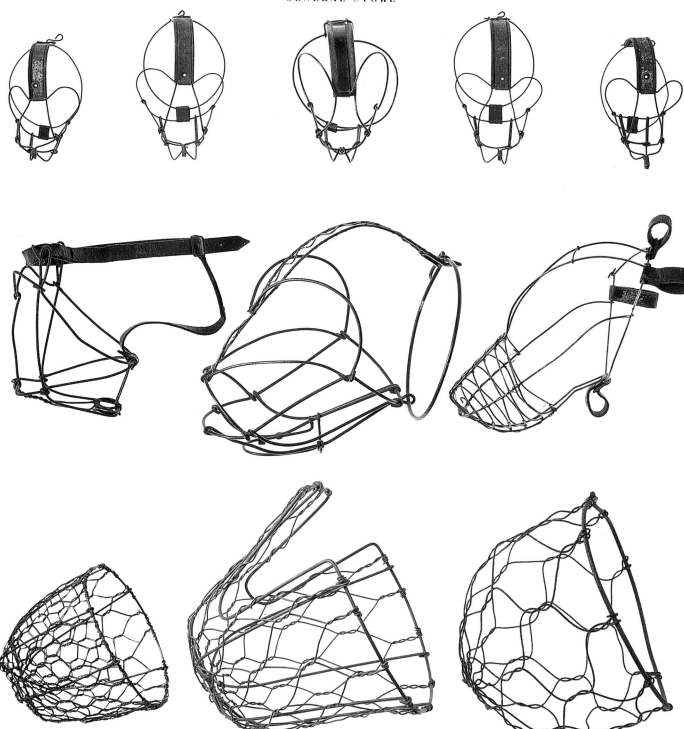

ABOVE Wire was a good material for fashioning muzzles for small monkeys, top row, for dogs, center row, and for calves and horses, bottom row.

RIGHT In the past Indian corn was dried on special wire hangers that were hung in the barn. The dried corn was used as animal fodder during the winter months. Today, the corn dryer adds an authentic touch to a country-style decor.

Many American agricultural tools were made of wire, including garden
forks and weeders and pear and apple pickers.

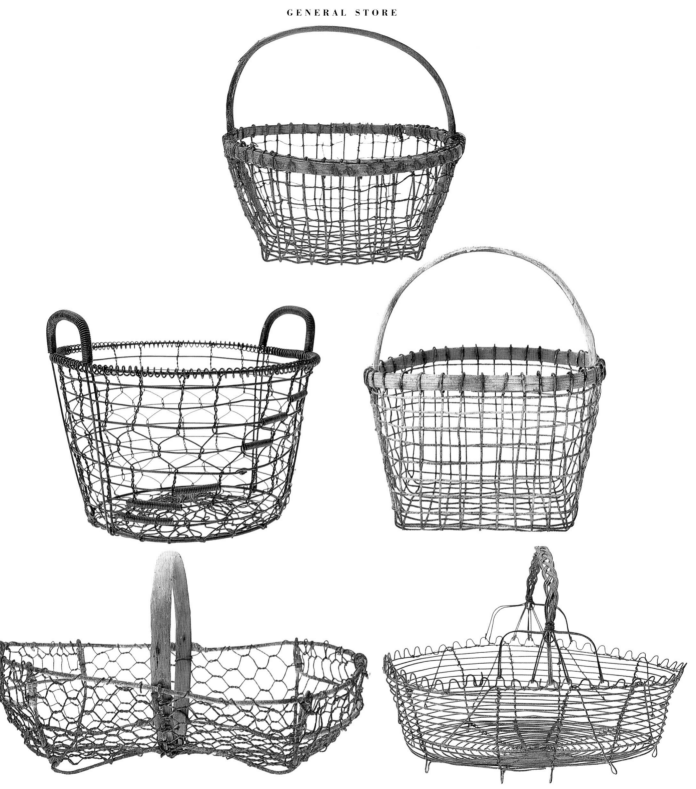

Large, sturdy baskets were used to carry clams from the seashore and
potatoes from the field.

ABOVE The day's catch was brought home in tall baskets made of flexible wire netting.

RIGHT On the dock of a small fishing village, oysters have been collected in a wire basket with a sturdy cord handle, while clams sit in a very large flat basket of wire woven tightly over a wood frame.

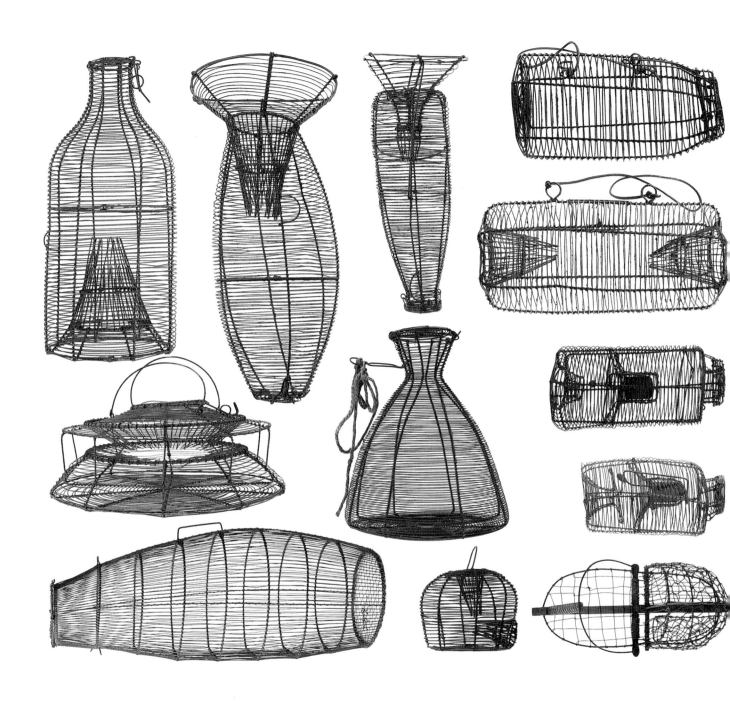

A wide variety of traps for mice and birds and nets for fish were made
of wire. Each was specifically designed for the particular prey, whether
turtle doves, eels, or crayfish.

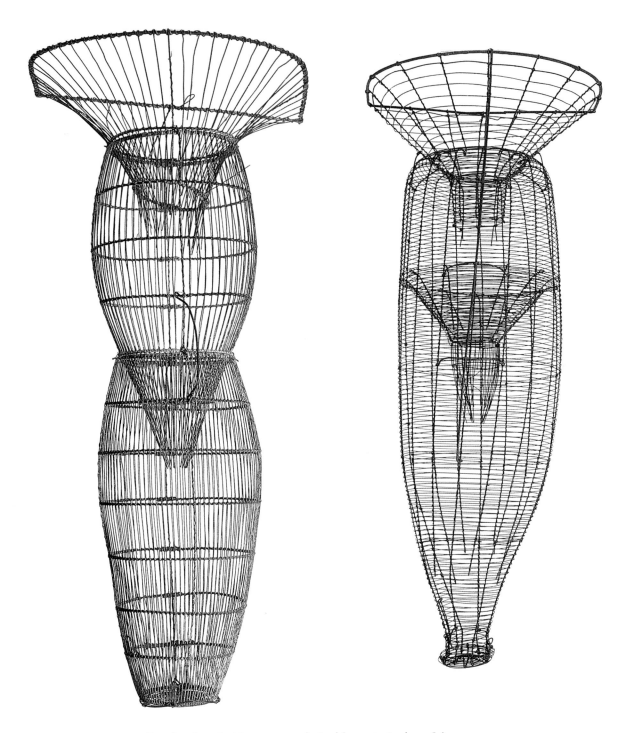

Four-foot-long double traps were devised for capturing large fish
and eels.

TOYS

In Europe, crafting toys especially for children was a tradition dating back to the Middle Ages. But it wasn't until the mid-nineteenth century that playthings that were both for fun and for learning began to be imported to the United States. American manufacturers quickly recognized their commercial potential, however, and applied the new technology to develop what promised to be a growth industry.

Of course, only children in very wealthy families were given expensive toys, including small-scale reproductions of the famous ships they had heard about or the fancy horse-drawn carriages with which they were familiar. Gender was respected: boys played with locomotives, trolley cars, and boats; girls were more interested in tea sets and doll beds and strollers.

Children in less privileged households had to be contented with toys that cost a fraction of the price of their deluxe counterparts. These were made of wood, papier mâché, tin, or in some cases cast iron. Many children made do with "toys" and games that required only a few rudimentary items: a piece of wood with a rubber band became a catapult; a bit of chalk and a ston were all that was needed to play hopscotch; and piece of cord transformed the pavement into an aren for jumping rope.

But as more sophisticated toys were manufacture and appeared in catalogs, even people of lesser mean wanted to give their children the toys they craved Especially at Christmas, shop windows were filled wit tantalizing new toys, and parents and children alik dreamed of owning them.

Wire allowed handmade versions of the profes sionally manufactured toys to be fashioned at home These toys, inspired by the circus, the country fair, th market, the kitchen, and the furniture of the perioc became the homespun folk-art version of the store bought variety.

Mainly because they were never made in quantit very few of these wire toys have survived. Most wer one-of-a-kind examples. Even though they were ofte made as special gifts, their fate was similar to that c most children's playthings.

RIGHT A wire carousel, once presented as a modest gift to a child, is now considered a recherché piece of folk art.

ABOVE In America the Ferris wheel was a popular subject for toys. Like the clockwork iron-and-steel version that became popular in the 1890s, the more rudimentary wire toy was also inspired by the World's Columbian Exposition of 1893 in Chicago.

RIGHT In the 1920s in France, children were particularly fond of wire puzzles that were packaged in amusing boxes with humorous cartoon-like illustrations.

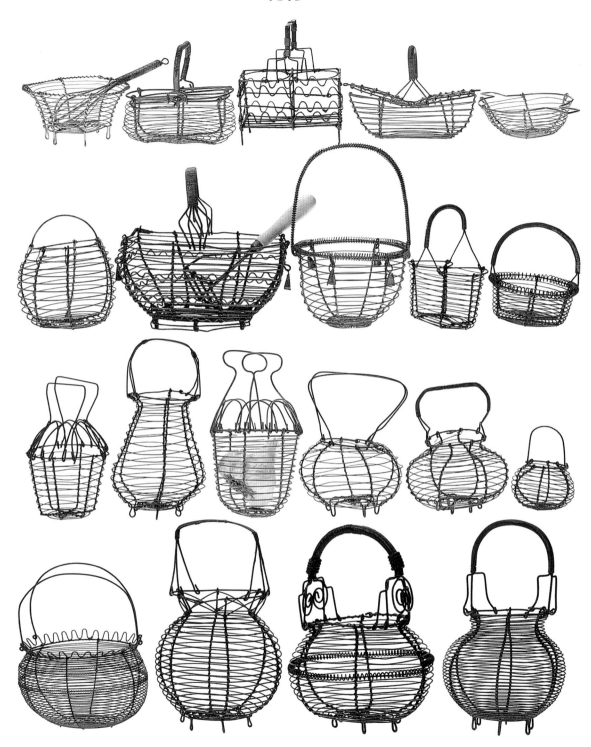

All the traditional wire accoutrements of the kitchen, such as salad and snail baskets, bottle carriers, eggbeaters, and potato mashers were miniaturized into wire toys.

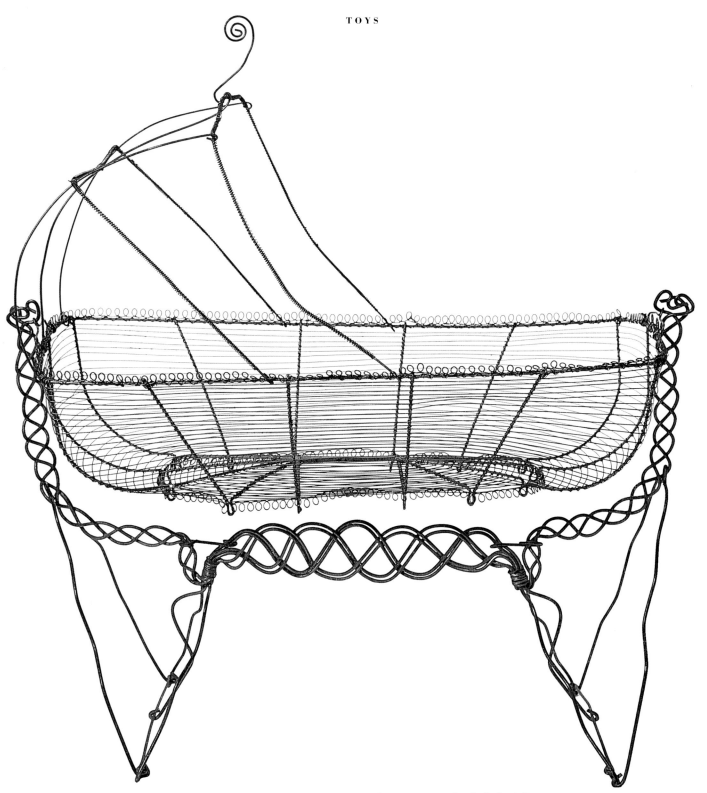

A wire bassinet that swings on its own frame was a staple of a little girl's nursery for her dolls.

Whether dolls were made of cloth or porcelain, little girls usually put them to sleep in wire beds and cradles that imitated the styles of the real-life furnishings of the second half of the nineteenth century. While the father or grandfather fashioned the frames, the mother sewed the mattress and bedclothes out of leftover bits of cloth, such as mattress ticking. The French rocking chair for a doll, top left, reflected the popularity of this type of furniture.

A pram for a large doll, crafted entirely of wire, probably dates from
the 1880s, when such carriages were considered necessary for taking
Baby out for long walks in the fresh air.

WIRE DIRECTORY

Antiques shows and flea markets are the places to look for antique wire things. *Antiques and The Arts Weekly,* published by the Bee Publishing Co., Newtown, Conn., is a good reference for shows in the United States, England, and France. A selection of antiques dealers who carry interesting wire pieces in the United States, Austria, England, Finland, France, Slovakia, and Sweden is listed below:

UNITED STATES

AMERICAN PRIMITIVE GALLERY
594 Broadway, Room 205
New York, NY 10012
(212) 966-1530

AMERICAN WING
Main Street
Bridgehampton, NY 11932
(516) 537-3319

KATHRYN BERENSON QUILTS
7206 Meadow Lane
Chevy Chase, MD 20815
(301) 718-0570

C.I.T.E.
100 Wooster St.
New York, NY 10012
(212) 431-7272

COUNTRY KITCHEN ANTIQUES
Mary and Bill Arciprete
Huntington, NY 11743
(516) 271-2238

ENGLISH COUNTRY ANTIQUES
Snake Hollow Road
Bridgehampton, NY 11932
(516) 537-0606

PAUL F. FULLER ANTIQUES
P.O. Box 441
Wiscasset, Maine 04578
(207) 832-5550

HENRO
525 Broome St.
New York, NY 10013
(212) 343-0221

HINTON & CO.
108 Wooster St.
New York, NY 10012
(212) 343-2430

HOPE & WILDER HOME
454 Broome St.
New York, NY 10013
(212) 966-9010

HULSEY-KELTER ANTIQUES
P.O. Box 213
Norfolk, CT 06058
(203) 542-1886

HOWARD KAPLAN ANTIQUES
827 Broadway
New York, NY 10003
(212) 674-1000

KELTER-MALCÉ
74 Jane St. (by appointment)
New York, NY 10014
(212) 989-6760

LAMBERTVILLE ANTIQUE MARKET
Route 29 So.
Lambertville, NJ
(609) 397-0456

DAVID M. MANCUSO ANTIQUES
6075 Rt. 202 & Upper Mt. Rd.
New Hope, PA 18938
(215) 794-5009

J. GARVIN MECKING
72 E. 11th St.
New York, NY 10003
(212) 677-4316

FRAN NESTOR
JOHN KRYNICK
P.O. Box 881
Lynn, MA 01903
(617) 596-1853

WIRE DIRECTORY

PANTRY & HEARTH
21 E. 35th St. (by appointment)
New York, NY 10016
(212) 532-0535

ROOMS & GARDENS
290 Lafayette St.
New York, NY 10012
(212) 431-1297
&
1631 Wisconsin Ave., N.W.
Washington, DC
(202) 965-3820

PAULA RUBENSTEIN
65 Prince St.
New York, NY 10012
(212) 966-8954

SAGE ST. ANTIQUES
Sage Street
Sag Harbor, NY 11963
(516) 725-4036

SAMMY'S
484 Broome St.
New York, NY 10013
(212) 343-2357

CAROLE SMYTH ANTIQUES
50 Youngs Hill Rd.
Huntington, NY 11713
(516) 673-8666

T & K FRENCH ANTIQUES, INC.
120 Wooster St.
New York, NY 10012
(212) 219-2472

PETER WERNER, LTD.
3709 South Dixie Highway
West Palm Beach, FL 33405
(407) 832-0428

AUSTRIA

BRIC A BRAC
Habsburgergasse 9
1010 Vienna
533-60-26

HARDY
Dorotheergasse 1h
1010 Vienna
512-18-05

LEOPOLDINE PRINZ
Dorotheergasse 6-8
1010 Vienna
512-47-19

ENGLAND

DECORATIVE PARLOR PIECES
82 Golborne Road
London W10 5PS
(081) 969-6262

JUDY GREENWOOD ANTIQUES
657 Fulham Road
London SW6 5PY
(071) 736-6037

INTERNATIONAL ANTIQUE &
COLLECTORS FAIR, LTD.
P.O. Box 100
Newark, Notts, NG24 4EQ
(0636) 702-326

SARA LEMKOW
12 Camden Passage
London N1 BES
(071) 359-0190

LENSON AND SMITH ANTIQUES
11 Church St.
London NW8 8EE
(071) 724-7763

MYRIAD
131 Portland Road
London W11 4LW
(071) 229-1709

PALMER ANTIQUES
7-8 Union St.
The Lanes
Brighton BN1 1H Sussex
(0273) 328-669

WIRE DIRECTORY

FINLAND

CASA MARIA
Korkkevuorenkatu 6
Helsinki
665-357

HILDAN JA HULDAN
Rauhankatu 6
Helsinki
628-877

POP ANTIK
Liisankatu 15
Helsinki
135-93-59

FRANCE

ART POPULAIRE
Marché Vernaison
93400 Saint-Ouen
40-11-19-10

AUTREFOIS
10 rue Ernest-Cresson
75014 Paris
45-40-61-63

BACHELIER
Marché Paul-Bert
18 rue Paul-Bert
93400 Saint-Ouen
45-06-59-39

HERVÉ BAUME
19 ter rue de la Petite-Fusterie
84000 Avignon
90-86-37-66

HUGUETTE BERTRAND
22, rue Jacob
75006 Paris
43-26-59-08

MICHEL BOUDIN
Marché Jules-Vallès
93400 Saint-Ouen

LE COCHELIN
Le Louvre des Antiquaires
2 place du Palais-Royal
75001 Paris
42-61-50-96

LES DEUX ORPHELINES
21 place des Vosges
75004 Paris
42-72-63-97

FANETTE
1 rue d'Alençon
75015 Paris
42-22-21-73

AU FOND DE LA COUR
49 rue de Seine
75006 Paris
43-25-81-89

LA GALERIE PITTORESQUE
Le Louvre des Antiquaires
2 place du Palais-Royal
75001 Paris
42-61-58-06

ELSA HALFEN
14 rue des Jardins-Saint-Paul
75004 Paris
48-87-13-54

L'HERMINETTE
Le Louvre des Antiquaires
2 place du Palais-Royal
75001 Paris
42-61-57-81

MARIE-NOELLE JACQUELIN
Marché Paul-Bert
93400 Saint-Ouen
40-12-88-31

MARIE CLAUDE PFENNIGER
Marché Paul-Bert
18 rue Paul-Bert
93400 Saint-Ouen
40-12-36-90

PATRICK MOLINA
Marché Vernaison
93400 Saint-Ouen
43-46-01-00

LA PETITE COUSINE
15 rue Gay Lussac
75005 Paris
43-26-36-59

WIRE DIRECTORY

ORTOBELLO
6 rue Notre-Dame-des-Champs
5006 Paris
3-35-74-47

ANNE VINCENT
1 boulevard Raspail
5007 Paris
0-49-02-21

MOUVEMENT JEUDI
2 rue Mouffetard
5005 Paris
3-31-44-52

LOVAKIA

ARTISAN
ybarska brana
ratislava
32-075

EVA HASIKOVA
Michalska 3
ratislava
31-578

ARAKY GALERIA
anska 17
ratislava
32-661

IRENA PISUTOVA
Prepostska 4
Bratislava
493-309

REX
Obchodna 12
Bratislava
335-655

STAROZITNOSTI
Majkova 2
Bratislava
219-498

SWEDEN

A LA CARTE
Linnegatan 22
S-114 47 Stockholm
08-661-99-88

SKATTGOMMAN
Skomakargatan 28
S-111 29 Stockholm
08-20-74-89

MORMORS SPEGEL
Odengatan 84
S-113 22 Stockholm

LOVISA ULRIKA
Kopmangatan 9
S-111 31 Stockholm
08-20-37-03

ACKNOWLEDGMENTS

We would like to thank all the people who supported and helped us along our wire adventure. They include: Philip Cutler; James Dupree, Patricia Lusk, and Pam Nelson at the Balch Institute for Ethnic Studies, Philadelphia; Jenny Eigen; Anna-Lena Einarsson; Alice Eisen; Zuzana Evrard-Bojnansky and Luc Evrard; Helaine and Burton Fendelman; Vladimir Ferko; Paul Grange; Muriel Grateau; Emily Gwathmey; Ian Hammond; Ladislav Jurovaty; Jolie Kelter and Michael Malcé; Jana Kopecka; Mariette Landon; Claude Lelieur and Claudine Chevrel of the Bibliothèque Forney, Paris; Gail Lettick; Catherine Levy and Agathe Mangelle of Scènes sur Seine; Marie-Jeanne and Marianne Ménard; Marian Mrva and Katarina Halonova of the Považské Museum, Žilina; Paola Navone; Suzanne Nazet; Stephen Pearse; Lazare Rozensztroch; Paula Rubenstein; Marc Schwartz; Jonathan Scott; Michael, Jake, and Lucie Steinberg; Selma Weiser; and Ingrid Zerunian.

Thank you also to our agents, Lucy Kroll and Barbara Hogenson, of the Lucy Kroll Agency; and to Abbeville Press in New York and Paris: Robert Abrams, Alan Mirken, Mark Magowan, Susan Costello, Marike Gauthier, and especially our editor, Jackie Decter.

INDEX

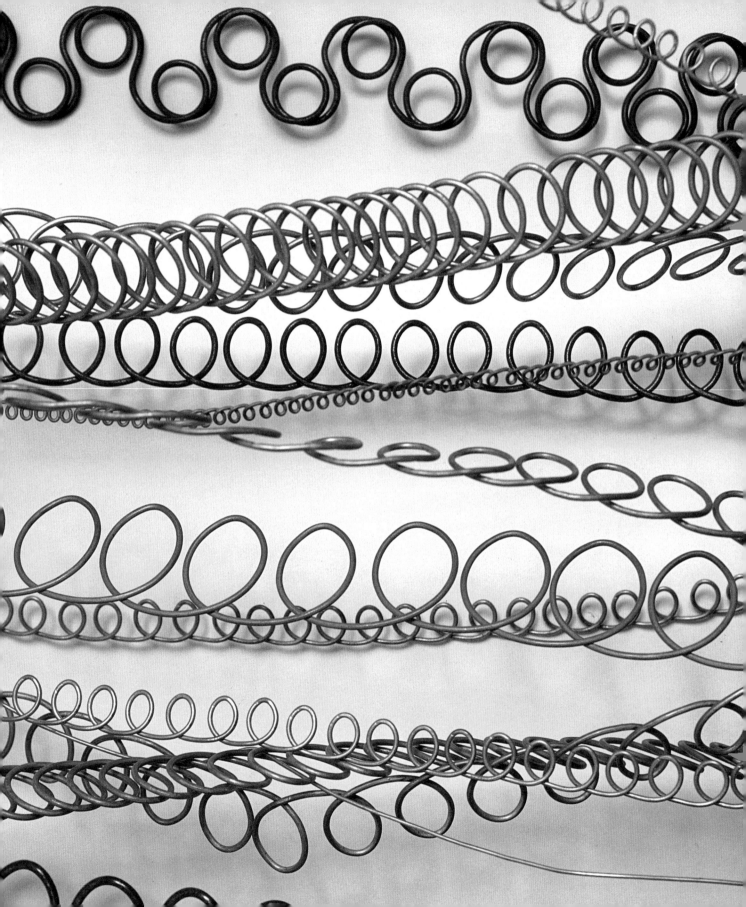